RISE
AND
ORGANISE

RISE

AND

ORGANISE

The Birth of
The Workers and National Movements
in Jamaica (1936-1939)

RICHARD HART

Rise And Organise:
The Birth Of The Workers And National
Movements In Jamaica (1936-39).

First Published in 1989 by Karia Press.
Copyright © Richard Hart, 1989.

Typeset by Karia.
Cover Design by Buzz Johnson

Printed and bound in Great Britain by
Biddles Ltd, Guildford and King's Lynn

ISBN 0 946918 72 4 Pb
ISBN 0 946918 73 2 Hb

Karia Press,
41, Rheola Close,
London, N17 9TR.
United Kingdom.

Contents

Dedicated to
Those who gave their lives and liberty
for progress.

Acknowledgments

As will be evident from the sources acknowledged, my own records and recollections have been supplemented by referring to contemporary newspaper reports and public records. For making these available I am indebted to the British Museum's newspaper library, The Institute of Jamaica and the Public Record Office in London. A special word of gratitude is due to Ken Post, upon whose work *Arise Ye Starvelings* I have relied for my quotations from the newspaper *Plain Talk* and other information. The photographs of street scenes in 1938 have been in my possession since that time and were, I believe, obtained from the late Charles Rhoden, a photographer thanks to whom this important part of the visual record has been preserved. This project has been realised on the initiative of Buzz Johnson of Karia Press.

Finally, I am grateful to my wife Avis for her infinite patience in typing and re-typing the manuscript, and indeed all my other manuscripts over the years, and assisting me in so many other ways.

Richard Hart,
London 1988

About The Author

Richard Hart, lawyer, historian, trade unionist and active participant in the progressive political activities of the Caribbean region, was born in Jamaica in August 1917. A founder-member of the Peoples National Party in 1938, he served on its Executive Committee until the ouster of its Marxist left wing in 1952.

A member of the Labour Committee arising out of the social upheaval in Jamaica in 1938, he acted as secretary of the Trade Union Advisory Committee (fore-runner of the T.U.C.) in 1939, helped organise railway workers in 1942, was President of the Jamaica Govt. Railway Employees Union, 1942-48 and a Vice-President of the T.U.C. until 1953. In 1942-43 he and others were imprisoned without trial by the colonial government.

Having represented the P.N.P. and T.U.C. at the founding conference of the Caribbean Labour Congress in Barbados in 1945, he was its Secretary from 1946 to 1953. 1953-57 he was legal adviser to the Sugar & Agricultural Workers Union in Jamaica and from 1954 to 1963 was a member of the Peoples Freedom Movement and its successor the Socialist Party of Jamaica.

He edited *The Mirror* newspaper in Guyana, 1964-65, coming to England in 1965. From 1965 to 1982 he worked in local government and was appointed Solicitor to a Local Authority in Surrey in 1968. A member of the National Association of Local Government Officers, he served on the Managing Committee of his local branch. But his main interest remained the Caribbean area and he was one of the founders in 1974 of Caribbean Labour Solidarity.

In 1982 he went to Grenada as Legal Adviser to the Peoples Revolutionary Government, becoming its Attorney General in May, 1983 and returning to Britain after the U.S. invasion. At the invitation of the P.N.P. he spoke at its Womens Rally in 1980 and participated in the election campaign. At the invitation of the Workers Party of Jamaica he spoke at its annual conference rally in 1984.

Author of a two volume work *Slaves Who Abolished Slavery,* published by the University of the W.I., and numerous booklets and pamphlets, he has lectured on Caribbean history and politics at universities and colleges in Britain, Canada, the U.S.A., Cuba and the Commonwealth Caribbean.

He is currently President of C.L.S. and an active member of the Committee for Human Rights in Grenada.

Introduction

It was while engaged in preparing an Introduction for the republication of Jamaica's first 'communist' newspaper, the *Jamaica Labour Weekly*, that the idea of writing this book occurred to me. That little newspaper, which made its first appearance on May 14, 1938 and its last in July 1939, was an important part of the popular awakening and a milestone in labour journalism. What has been attempted here is an account, if not the whole at least of the most important aspects, of that awakening; to identify the factors contributing to the upheaval; and to show how the first foundations were laid at that time for the trade union and political organisations which exist today. An important element in this process was the Marxist contribution, the origins and early development of which have been here recorded.

One

Days Compressing
Twenty Years

Back in the 1930s, when Charles Darwin had already achieved
posthumous respectability, and the use of Karl Marx's name to frighten
people was just beginning in the English-speaking Caribbean, it was
not uncommon for pseudo-intellectuals to say: 'I believe in evolution
not revolution'. A more inept comparison would be difficult to imagine,
for evolution and revolution have never been alternatives. As Marx so
clearly demonstrated: though the factors making for social progress
mature gradually, progress makes itself evident in a series of sudden
leaps and bounds. Evolution manifests itself in a succession of
revolutions. In a letter to his friend Frederick Engels Marx once
wrote:

> In developments of such magnitude twenty years are [no] more
> than a day — though later on days may come again compressing
> twenty years.[1]

This is precisely what happened in the British colonies of the Caribbean area. The wave of working class unrest which, in the wake of the
1914-18 War, swelled across the region, had everywhere subsided in the
1920s. But although the impoverishment of the masses had steadily
increased, exacerbated by the effects of the world capitalist crisis
which commenced at the end of 1929 and lasted well into the 1930s,
there had been little or no indication of the depth of popular
dissatisfaction.

Elsewhere a description of the situation in the 1930s has been given
in the following terms:

> What appeared on the surface was a picture of general working
> class subservience and docility. Surveying the scene, colonial
> officials, representatives of the big foreign owned enterprises and
> the local employers, and upper middle classes generally felt confi-

13

dent and secure. Those who interpreted the situation differently, like the visiting professor W.M. Macmillan, whose book *Warning from the West Indies* was first published in Britain in February 1936, were dismissed as alarmists or trouble-makers. Sullen resentment and dissatisfaction were, nevertheless, swelling steadily among the working people and the unemployed in all the British colonies of the Caribbean area. By the middle years of the decade the situation was like a cauldron of liquid slowly coming to the boil, with isolated early warning bubbles here and there disturbing the apparently placid surface.[2]

The apparent subservience of the black masses towards those above them on the social scale — the predominantly white or brown upper and middle classes — was sufficiently widespread to create doubts as to whether the workers would ever gain the self-confidence and class consciousness required to challenge the established order. The prevailing standards of value also affected the intelligensia. The top administrative posts in state, church and industry were, for the most part, reserved for persons sent out to the colonies from Britain. Local Whites or light-complexioned persons, who related socially to the expatriates, were, however, admitted to the upper echelons of the Colonial Civil Service[3] or managerial bureaucracy in business. But so firmly established was the understanding that the top people would always be white, or as near thereto as possible, that the appointment in the 1940s of the first black Anglican Archbishop of Jamaica occasioned considerable surprise, and that despite his obvious 'respectability' and well-known conservatism.[4]

The upheavals of the 1930s affected almost the entire English-speaking Caribbean area. In colony after colony there were days in which, as Marx had said, the developments of the last twenty years suddenly found expression. The social explosion commenced in Belize (then British Honduras) in 1934 followed by a second explosion in the small eastern Caribbean island of St. Kitts in 1935. Later that same year St. Vincent erupted. Though in 1936 a similar upheaval in St. Lucia was prevented by an intimidatory display of imperial might, social explosions followed in Barbados and in Trinidad and Tobago in 1937, and in Jamaica in 1938. In 1938 and 1939 widespread strikes and social unrest occurred in British Guiana.

For the revised edition of his book, republished in 1938 after most of these events had occurred, Professor Macmillan wrote a preface in which he included this polite 'I told you so':

When I went to the West Indies I was told by men of all shades of opinion that I should find everything ideal and fully expected to. My doubts when I returned were received coldly.[5]

Prior to the events of the 1930s, it had been the policy of British capitalists with substantial investments in the colonies, and the big local employers, to oppose the organisation of their employees into trade unions. In this they had enjoyed the support of the colonial officials whose principal task it was to protect their interests. Not only were organisational activities obstructed and strikers habitually harassed by the police, but trade union legislation, grudgingly enacted to placate unrest, did not authorise peaceful picketing or provide immunity for trade unions from liability for actions in tort or breach of contract.[6]

The social explosions of the 1930s compelled the principal employers and the colonial establishments to reappraise their traditional strategy of hostility to the organisation of labour. Having witnessed the extent to which spontaneous unorganised strikes and riots could destroy property and endanger life, the capitalists and their representatives were forced to the conclusion, though not without difficulty in some individual cases, that collective bargaining with 'responsible' trade union leaders was a lesser evil. Once that decision had been reached, the term 'responsible' quickly came to mean 'corruptible'.

Two

The First Trade Unions

Prior to the 1930s there had been two periods of trade union organisation in Jamaica. The earlier period commenced with the organisation of
the first of the unions of artisans in 1898 and developed further with the
first unions of printers and cigar makers in 1907. But before the start of
the 1914-18 War all these unions were defunct. The second period commenced towards the end of World War I with the formation of another
cigar makers union in 1916 and was greatly strengthened in the
immediate postwar period when waterfront workers, railway workers,
hotel workers and others were organised. But again, in the 1920s, all
these unions ceased to exist. An attempt to organise another union in
1929 had failed by 1931.

The third period of trade union organisation in Jamaica started with
the formation of the Jamaica Workers and Tradesmen Union
(J.W.T.U.) in 1936. The founders of this organisation were Alan George
St. Claver Coombs and Hugh Clifford Buchanan. Coombs, a powerfully
built former soldier and policeman, came from the parish of St. Ann. In
a letter to a local newspaper he described himself as 'a peasant of low
birth, very limited education and a very poor man'.[7] His departure from
the police force was said to have been a consequence of his defiance of a
white officer whom he bested when they came to blows. He could be
described as a natural radical but had no theoretical motivation.

Buchanan, a master brick mason, was a remarkable man. He was
born on January 29, 1907. At the age of twelve, unable to get on with a
domineering father, he left his home at May Pen and went to live with
his aunt at Dias in Hanover. He migrated with her to Cuba at the age of
sixteen.[8] In Cuba he learned his trade, in which he attained a high
degree of proficiency. The date of his return is not known but he was in
Jamaica in 1929.

16

It is unlikely that he was directly engaged in political activities during the time he was living in Cuba. Nevertheless the evident self-respect of the Cuban people impressed him and this undoubtedly helped him to rise above the colonial mentality which affected most of his fellow countrymen at that time. In a letter to the progressive news magazine *Public Opinion,* of December 18, 1937, he wrote:

> The illiterate Cuban guajiro beats his breast with pride and declares: 'I am a Cuban' . . . The pride of even the most illiterate Cuban is due to the fact that at a certain time in the past they rose and did something monumental. The deeds of a Maceo, a Marti and a thousand patriots who distinguished themselves in the struggle are written in prose, and poetry, and in the text books of their schools. It is the source of a never ending folklore, the vital chord to which every Cuban responds. 'La independencia' even though reduced to a solemn farce by the strangle-hold of Wall Street, is nevertheless the motive force, the ideal of a nation of progressive people less than one hundred miles from us.[9]

Shortly after the formation of the J.W.T.U. a few other trade unions came into existence. The Builders and Allied Trade Union had started as the artisans' section of the J.W.T.U. but had hived off early in 1938 to become a separate organisation. Its principal leader was Percy A. Aiken who, as chargeman-electrician at the Railway, had been one of the leaders of the railway workers' strike of 1919 and the short-lived union that grew out of it. In the 1930s he had his own electrician workshop in Kingston, with two or three apprentices.

In 1937 shop assistants and store clerks in Kingston had been organised into the Jamaica United Clerks Association with F.A. Glasspole, an accountant employed to the merchant S.N. Shoucair, as Secretary, and a barrister, Erasmus Campbell, as President. Also in 1937 or early 1938, Ken Hill, a *Gleaner* reporter, had played a prominent part in the formation of the Motor Omnibus Drivers Association. Hill was also associated with a small chauffeurs' union.[10]

Three

The Marxist Pioneers

Buchanan was Jamaica's first active Marxist. The person who introduced him to communist ideas was Cleveland Antonio King, a Jamaican who had resided in Cuba for many years and may indeed have grown up there. I recall that, after I had known King for some time, his mother and sister and his sister's husband returned from Cuba. King had been a member of the illegal Cuban Communist Party at the time when Julio Antonio Mella was its General Secretary. On his return to Jamaica he at first followed his trade as a tile maker, though he later started a small box-making factory. Their work in the building trade had brought King and Buchanan together.[11]

Buchanan was an avid reader and there was not much, if anything, the King could do to help him with reading material. But, possibly through his letters to the newspapers, Buchanan had attracted the attention of a man who had a good library of Marxist works. This was Audley Thomas, a senior civil servant in the Colonial Secretary's Office. Though Thomas was a convinced Marxist-Leninist, he took no part in political activities. Despite this, the Colonial Secretary appears to have received a report concerning his sympathies and, as a consequence, he was transferred to a less politically sensitive post in the Department of Education.

Thomas was always having to take work home and believed that he was deliberately over-loaded with office responsibilities so as to ensure that he would have no time to do anything else. He lived alone and led a very quiet life, and was always glad of visit from Buchanan or myself. I believe it was from him that Buchanan first obtained a copy of Lenin's *The State and Revolution,* and Buchanan in turn introduced this important work to me.

18

In an earlier letter to *Public Opinion* published on July 3, 1937, Buchanan had deplored the 'deliberate renunciation of the economic and political struggle by poor people in Jamaica' which, he pointed out:

> reflects itself chiefly in the rise and multiplication of Lodges, Burial and Benevolent Societies, political and religious superstitions and deliberate fraud and roguery. The philosophy of the Benevolent and Burial Societies is: instead of standing united to cast off and reject undue social and economic burdens, and striving for social and political readjustments, they passively and mutually agree to distribute the shock among themselves pro rata.

In this situation, the letter continued, the only 'methods of struggle' in use were that:

> We wreak vengeance through petty larceny and bad debts upon members of the community, equally poor and oppressed as ourselves; through religious intoxications we defer the need of a decent, well cared for existence until the Second Coming, and we mutually agree to absorb the burden, whatever it may be.[12]

I was first attracted to Buchanan by his letters, giving the 'communist' point of view, which were occasionally published in the *Daily Gleaner*. In those days the *Gleaner* had not yet developed its policy of confining what it published about Marxism and 'communism' mainly to hostile misrepresentations. When, early in 1937, he was pointed out to me at one of the formative meetings of the National Reform Association (mentioned below), I nominated him for the Managing Council. From that time on we became friends and comrades. Later that same year, Jamaica's first Marxist group, loosely centred around Buchanan, began to meet.

The original members of this group were Buchanan, Wellesley A. McBean, Frank Hill, Albreath A. Morris, T.G. Christian, Cecil Nelson, Lionel Lynch and myself. Some time later, I think in 1938, we were joined by Osmond Dyce and Henry Fowler, and early in 1939 by Arthur Henry. McBean used to make his living by importing, roasting and selling peanuts in packets. To his modest stock he later added progressive publications and Left Book Club books. Frank Hill, Ken's younger brother, was a journalist who had worked on the *Daily Mail* which was no longer published. He was one of the three founders, in 1937, of the news magazine *Public Opinion*. Morris and Christian were tally clerks on the wharves. There were six tally clerks who all lived at the same boarding house, which became known as 'Moscow' because they often met to listen to Radio Moscow. Radios were not very common in those days. Nelson was apprenticed to Buchanan to learn the mason's trade, but did not persevere in this and in 1938 became a union office messenger. Osmond Dyce was a sheet metal worker whom I recruited one Sunday when selling pamphlets along Gold Street in Kingston.

Lynch was a longshoreman and stevedore. He received his introduction to Marxism while resident in the U.S.A., through the writings and speeches of the then leader of the Communist Party, Earl Browder. He also recalled being influenced by the writings of Corlis Lamont. On returning to Jamaica in the early 1930s he was employed as a stevedore in Port Antonio and became the Secretary of the Eastern Portland Citizens Association. A guest speaker at the Kencot Citizens Association, a newspaper report of his speech attracted the attention of William Alexander Bustamante, about whom I shall have much to say below. Bustamante was then associated with the Jamaica Workers and Tradesmen's Union and the up-shot of their meeting was that Lynch participated with Bustamante in a public meeting at Port Antonio in 1936, which cost him his job along with seventeen others. He then moved to Kingston, getting a job as a stevedore at the Princess Street Wharf.[13]

Lynch's first contact with our Marxist group was through Frank Hill and myself at the office and printery of *Public Opinion* on Temple Lane. I vividly recall a Friday night in 1937 when the electric motor that drove the little press broke down and it was Lynch to the rescue. A powerful man, he stood there for hours turning the fly-wheel of the press so that the printing of the paper could be completed.

Fowler was the son of a planter and had had little or no contact with the working class. Having won the Jamaica Scholarship he had become a Marxist at Oxford University where he had been elected President of the Oxford Union. Arthur Henry was probably much the same age as Buchanan. He had been a railway fitter who had later gone to sea as an engine room oiler on the Canadian 'Lady' boats. I was then a nineteen-year-old law student, articled to my father's senior partner in the firm of Manton and Hart. During 1939 we admitted many others to our ranks.[14]

Four

Other Formative Influences

On the eve of the events of 1938, in addition to the tributaries to the modern trade union movement which have been mentioned, other contributory streams were flowing which might be described as currents of intellectual ferment. Some of these, which deserve to be included among the contemporary formative influences, are mentioned below.

Plain Talk, a weekly newspaper edited by veteran Garvey supporter Alfred Mends, had started publication in 1935 (or possibly late 1934). Mends was a politician in the populist mould who sought to give expression to the sentiments of the little man. In the columns of his paper he expressed concern for the welfare of the masses and advocated the interests of natives as against foreigners, particularly with relation to the small businessman. *Plain Talk* devoted much space to the invasion of Ethiopia by Italy under Mussolini, a cause of grave popular concern in Jamaica. Somehow the paper succeeded in giving its readers a feeling of participation in defending Africa against this latest example of oppression by the white man. By no means an erudite publication, it was, in the mid 1930s, the voice of the people, but more a voice of protest than a purveyor of new ideas or concrete proposals.

The Kingston and St. Andrew Literary and Debating Society was, as its name implies, designed to be harmlessly diversionary. Nevertheless, some of its debates were on subjects of social significance and it provided an opportunity for the expression of many progressive ideas. It attracted and provided a training, or rather exercise, ground for potential orators, some of whom, like Ken Hill, went on to speak to more practical purpose politically.

In Kingston at this time there were several street orators, most of whom were known as 'political touts'. That term implied that they were for hire as speakers on the platforms of candidates standing in elections to the Legislative Council or the municipality — the Kingston and St. Andrew Corporation Council. But some of these men would also hold street meetings outside of election periods, just to express their views on various topics. The only remuneration they obtained from such efforts would have been the collections taken up from the audience, but as this was before the introduction of public address systems, their expenses would have been negligible. Such meetings provided opportunities for protesting against a variety of current concerns such as dominance of the retail grocery trade by Chinese shopkeepers or the growing volume of the dry goods trade controlled by the Lebanese, then known as 'Syrians'.

One of these street orators, who as far as I know was not a 'tout', was St. William Grant, who had been a member of Marcus Garvey's Universal Negro Improvement Association in New York. He spoke nightly from his portable rostrum at North Parade in Kingston. His favourite subject was the greatness of Africa's past. Being illiterate, he was unable to research the facts but he compensated for this by a fertile imagination and enthralled his audience with accounts of the exploits of warrior kings. In 1938 he was sharing his platform with William Alexander Bustamante who spoke of more immediate issues.

At a more sophisticated level there was the weekly news magazine *Public Opinion,* which started publication in February 1937. Osmond Theodore Fairclough, The Managing Editor, had lived in Haiti for some years where he had held a responsible position in the National Bank. Having become accustomed to seeing black men like himself in the highest positions of authority, the contrast when he returned to Jamaica in 1934 was gallingly evident. He presented his credentials to the managers of two commercial banks. At that time all the clerical and supervisory staff in the commercial banks were white or light complexioned. One of these managers declined to employ him without comment, but the other, somewhat apologetically, said that the only job he could offer him was that of a porter!

Two others who were associated with Fairclough in launching *Public Opinion* were Frank Hill and Hedley P. Jacobs. Hill, as we have seen, was a journalist. Jacobs was a scholarly English liberal who had come to Jamaica as a teacher in 1925 and had settled. Incidentally, he married Audley Thomas' sister. *Public Opinion* became a forum for the expresion of advanced ideas — advanced, that is, by comparison with the

22

prevailing imperialist and racist concepts which had so successfully permeated the whole of Jamaican society. Its columns were open to any progressive ideas its contributors might care to express. In particular, it was host to expressions of the growing nationalist sentiment and to anti-imperialist ideas across a wide spectrum, from bourgeois nationalism to Marxism.

A few months after the launching of the paper a small printing press was acquired and the offices of the paper at Temple Lane became, more than ever, a centre for lively discussion. This was particularly so every Friday night, as contributors and well-wishers gathered to help fold the pages and assemble and dispatch the paper as it came off the press. There were occasions when the work, and the discussions, went on right through the night, some of us going directly to work next morning without any sleep. The five-day week was unknown in 1937!

The intellectual ferment of the times was also affecting Jamaicans living in New York, U.S.A., where, in 1936, the Jamaica Progressive League (J.P.L.) had been formed. The purpose of the founders of the League — Wilfred A. Domingo, Jaime O'Meally, W. Adolphe Roberts and Rev. Ethelred Brown — was to stimulate and pursue a demand for self-government for Jamaica. Domingo and O'Meally, who had earlier been supporters of Marcus Garvey, had developed their anti-imperialism on the basis of Marxist-Leninist theory. Roberts and Brown had probably not gone much beyond the anti-colonialist ideals of most Americans. In 1937 the J.P.L. sent Roberts and Domingo to Jamaica where, to their pleasant surprise, they discovered that a lively interest in self-determination already existed.

In March 1937 Ken Hill took the initiative in launching a mildly nationalistic organisation called the National Reform Association (N.R.A.). Hill had sought some very 'respectable' sponsors and had persuaded C.G.X. Henriques, a young barrister who had just returned from England with an impeccable Oxford accent, to accept the presidency. At one of the early meetings of the N.R.A., which I shall never forget, the proceedings were interrupted by the arrival of St. William Grant, who invaded the hall with a substantial part of the audience from one of his street meetings. Advancing towards the platform, Grant demanded to know whether the leaders of this new organisation were 'prepared to die for the masses'. After a moment of confusion, an insurance company manager by the name of George Bowen, stepped boldly forward and declared: 'The answer to that question is YES!' But

23

dying for the masses was the last thing that many of the gentlemen on the platform had in mind. I do not recall ever seeing our worthy president at another meeting of the N.R.A. His place was taken by N.N. Nethersole, a solicitor, who became First Vice President of the People's National Party when it was formed in the following year.

The name of Norman Washington Manley is well known in Jamaica as the founder of the People's National Party, but in 1937, when he was the island's leading barrister, he was yet to be convinced that Jamaica's problems required a political solution. Fairclough told me that when he first approached Manley with the idea of forming a political party, Manley told him that Jamaica's problems were economic, not political. This was the view Manley put forward when he addressed the Jewish Literary Society in the last week of May 1937. *Public Opinion* reported part of what he said:

> It is idle to talk about political constitutions and political reforms. These things will inevitably come when we have social unity; and that will only come when our secondary schools have produced a sufficient number of persons to make an organic whole of the country.[15]

Writing under the pen-name 'Observer' in the same issue of *Public Opinion,* H.P. Jacobs exposed the inconsistency of this position:

> Mr. Manley held that politics were a negligible factor, but that Jamaica needed an educated class with a definite outlook on the social and economic problems which are so much more important than politics here. This overlooks the fact that any social outlook worth having is going to translate itself into action of some kind, and that such action is normally political, so that Mr. Manley was really urging that children should be taught the bases of political action, but not encouraged to regard political action as necessary.

The need to form a political party and what kind of party it should be was the subject of a lively debate in the columns of *Public Opinion* from December 1937 to April 1938, a debate in which Fairclough, Roberts, Domingo, O'Meally, Buchanan, W.A. McBean and I participated. But it was not until April or May 1938 that Fairclough finally persuaded Manley that a political party was a necessity and that he (Manley) should play the leading role in its formation.

24

Five

Peasant Unrest Develops

Parallel with the expressions of dissatisfaction which were increasing among the wage earners, and the aspirations which were stirring among the urban middle classes, unrest was also developing among the peasantry. Peasants constituted a large percentage of those engaged in agriculture in Jamaica. When the first modern census was taken in December 1942, 221,376 persons were found to be gainfully occupied in agriculture. Of these 127,659 were identified as wage earners and unpaid workers, 74,784 as own — account workers and 18,933 as employers.[16] Of the latter it can be assumed that the majority of these 'employers' worked alongside their employees in the fields. It would be safe to say that the peasantry comprised about forty percent of those gainfully employed in agriculture.

There was also a considerable over-lap between small farmers and estate labourers. Of the 66,173 farmers working farms of one acre or more, 21,927 or 33.1% did on average seventeen and a half weeks work off their own farms in 1942, mostly as agricultural labourers. When we take into consideration only the one-acre farms, the percentage working off their own farms during the year was nearly fifty percent.[17]

Likewise, a very large percentage of those classified as agricultural labourers, obtained at least some of their food or income from the cultivation of small plots of land which they either owned or rented. Holdings of less than one acre were not classified as farms by the Census. There were 138,425 such plots of land outside of Kingston in 1942 which produced agricultural products valued at less than £15.[18] A study conducted by the Labour Department in 1944 concluded that 'five out of every ten field workers possessed one acre of land' which they cultivated in between their estate work.[19]

Some indication of growing economic distress among the peasantry is contained in the increasing number of peasants imprisoned for non payment of taxes after 1935. The number so imprisoned in 1934-35 was fifty-seven, but this rose to one hundred and sixteen in 1935-36 and to one hundred and fifty-three in 1936-37.[20]

As Ken Post has noted, peasant dissatisfaction and disillusionment often manifest themselves in millenarianism and other forms of mystical or religious expression. In St. Thomas peasant disillusionment with prevailing institutions, standards of value and structures of property ownership had found expression in the early 1930s with the appearance of the Rastafarian cult under the leadership of Leonard Howell. But in 1935, from the same parish, came manifestations of more secular peasant concerns.

From Golden Grove in St. Thomas in November 1935 came a demand for land, in the traditional form of a petition to the Governor.[21] However, the first signatory to the petition, Dorrell Reid, had begun to show his discontent a few months earlier by writing letters to *Plain Talk* anticipating Armageddon and the Second Coming of Christ.[22]

At first the petitioners had sought to enlist the support of Rudolph Ehrenstein, the owner of Serge Island sugar estate who was also a member of the Legislative Council. But by shortly before Christmas 1935 it is evident,from the wording of a second petition, that they were recognizing the large land-owners as their oppressors:

> Your Excellency; we respectfully beg to inform you that quite a large number of us who rented lands from the big proprietors, when our products is in good condition and [we are] in any slight differences [with the proprietors] we are told to leave the land with the products thereon. Sir, this is painful, so we are asking for a good security against such evil visitation which often destroys our future prospect.[23]

A week later the petitioners formed the Tax and Rate-payers Association. Reid's letter to *Plain Talk* announcing its formation called on his fellow farmers 'to unite as one body of men and march in a great Army against this land parasite which is a stumbling block in our way especially we the poorer coloured race'. But although they had recognized the antagonistic interests of small farmers and big land owners and were now advancing to the level of organisation, these peasants still harboured illusions of the benevolent role of the colonial governor. Stressing the need for land, work and agricultural education the letter called for official assistance:

26

... our hands are tied standing in front of a deep gulf. But we can't stand there to starve and die, we must call to Government for help.[24]

A year later, discouraged by the lack of response from Government, the Association had progressed at least to the point of repudiating the Legislative Council:

> We are not to allow others who do not see our needs and cares to guide us. We cannot very well leave ourselves to Legislatures who nickname as Ambassadors to Govt. We can be Ambassadors if we will make up our minds to swell the members roll of the T & R P A of St. Thomas.[25]

A parallel and perhaps more significant peasant movement was meanwhile developing in the central parish of Clarendon under the leadership of a remarkable man, Robert E. Rumble. A poor peasant, Rumble had also acquired the trade of a coach-builder and wheelwright and had gone to Cuba in 1920 to work in the cane fields, returning to Jamaica in 1932.[26]

In February 1937 Rumble wrote to *Plain Talk* calling for someone to 'help us from the oppression of these iron-handed landowners in these parts of Clarendon'. More radical than his St. Thomas counterparts, he declared: 'We want no more landlords'. Two weeks later he wrote:

> We are under the hands of landlords for over ninety years now, and I think it is time that we should get governmental aids. We have carried this burden for a long time, but oh, we are sick, almost mad; can't we be remembered for once, or are we going to die in the poor house for want of governmental help.[27]

At first Rumble appears to have believed that the Jamaica Agricultural Society, an organisation which received an annual government grant and employed trained agricultural officers to advise farmers, could be made to serve the interests of the peasantry. In a letter published on April 3, 1937, he advised farmers to 'join the Jamaica Agricultural Society and buy a copy of *Plain Talk* every Saturday'. But later he came to the conclusion that small farmers needed their own organisation and formed the Poor Man's Improvement Land Settlement and Labour Association (P.M.I.L.S.L.A.), of which he was President and for which in March 1938 he claimed a membership of eight hundred.[28]

Given the close identification of the peasantry with the working class and the considerable over-lapping that existed in Jamaica, forms

27

of joint worker-peasant activity were a natural development. It is not surprising therefore that Rumble and his organisation should have emerged in upper Clarendon as representative of both the peasants and land hungry agricultural labourers. On April 23, 1938, the P.M.I.L.S.L.A. addressed a petition to the Governor which stated:

> We are the Sons of slaves who have been paying rent to the Landlords for fully many decades we want better wages, we have been exploited for years and we are looking to you to help us. We want a Minimum Wage Law. We want freedom in this the hundredth year of our Emancipation. We are still economic Slaves, burdened in paying rent to Landlords who are sucking out our vitalities.[29]

The demand for land found expression at this time in two directions. There was a movement by land hungry persons to occupy estate lands. A number of persons were arrested for occupying land at Trout Hall and Cocoa Walk. At the same time tenants were refusing to pay any more rent to the big land owners. The action taken by peasants of upper Clarendon is referred to below.

Six

The J.W.T.U. And Bustamante

Let us now return to the story of working class organisation. A.G.S. Coombs and Buchanan, who were pressing on with the pioneering task of organising an island-wide trade union and concentrating their efforts in the rural parishes, were encountering considerable financial difficulties. They had very little money and the cost of travelling was presenting a formidable problem. It was in this situation that they decided to turn for assistance to a public spirited individual by the name of William Alexander Bustamante. Born with the more prosaic surname Clarke, the latter may have adopted the name Bustamante while he was living in Cuba or Panama. He had returned to Jamaica from New York in 1934 and set up in business as a money lender.[30] A prolific writer of letters to the newspapers, he soon established a reputation for being willing to lend his support publicly to any popular cause. More important, from the Union's point of view, he owned a motor car.

Bustamante agreed to join the Jamaica Workers and Tradesmen's Union in 1936, initially as Treasurer. Soon, however, he demanded that he be made the President, but that created difficulties as Coombs was already President. Buchanan told me subsequently that it was he who had devised a solution acceptable to both men. Coombs was to remain President while for Bustamante a new office was to be created — President General! I am not aware of any documentary evidence that this plan was actually implemented.

During 1937 Bustamante made several organising trips to the rural areas with Coombs and Buchanan, but in the latter part of the year he became disenchanted with trade unionism. The problem was that his union activities were not getting the publicity he had expected, due to the *Gleaner's* policy at that time of giving very little publicity to attempts to organise the workers. Also there was friction with Coombs, who never fully relinquished his claim to the leadership. Eventually, in November 1937, though the details of their parting are not entirely clear, Bustamante severed his connections with the Union. Coombs, however, claimed that he had been expelled.

At the end of December 1937 there was unrest at Serge Island sugar estate in St. Thomas, at the eastern of the island, where the unorganised workers were demanding higher wages. In the first week of January 1938 the workers were on strike and Bustamante introduced himself there in a new role. No longer a trade union leader, he offered his services as a 'mediator' between capital and labour. This did get a headline in the *Gleaner* and the employer, Rudolph Ehrenstein, accepted his offer. But when Bustamante told the strikers how much the employer was willing to pay, they vigorously rejected his intervention. To quell the ensuing unrest, police from Kingston were brought into the area and a number of arrests were made. The owner offered further concessions directly to the workers and they returned to work.

Seven

Starvation Wages

As no cost of living statistics were recorded in Jamaica prior to 1939, it is difficult to say to what extent prices of necessities had risen since the 1920s. There had, however, been no parallel upward movement of wages.Though the profitability of sugar production had been somewhat improved as a result of the granting of increased imperial preferences in 1932 and 1934 and the introduction of the local subsidy provided under the terms of the *Sugar Industry Aid Law* of 1929, none of this had been passed on to the workers. It would not be an exaggeration to describe the prevailing rates as starvation wages. At the same time the spread of plant diseases had seriously reduced the incomes derived by full and part-time peasants from the growing of bananas.

No comprehensive statistics relating to wage rates or workers' weekly earnings in 1938 are available and rates of pay were not uniform throughout the island. Some information of prevailing wage levels can, however, be gleaned from evidence submitted to the West Indies Royal Commission which visited the island in November 1938, about which I shall have more to say later. The following table of estimated average daily rates of wages paid to labourers and artisans is from a memorandum prepared for the Colonial Government by G.H. Scott, the newly employed Unemployment and Wage Rates Officer, and submitted to the Commission.[31]

As we have now become accustomed to a decimalised currency and to thinking in dollars and cents, it may be as well to add the reminder that, when introduced, the Jamaican dollar was worth ten shillings. Thus (disregarding subsequent devaluations as irrelevant) the equivalent of one shilling (1/-) would have been ten cents , one penny (1d) would have been less than one cent.

(Extracted from memorandum prepared by G.H. Scott — presented by Govt. of Jamaica)

Showing Average wages paid Artisans and Labourers at the Public Works Department as compared with private employers at stated periods . . .

Type Of Employee		KINGSTON								OTHER PARISHES (Average)							
		Public Works Dept.				Private Employers				Public Works Dept.				Private Employers			
		1932	1937	1938 (a)	1938 (b)	1932	1937	1938 (a)	1938 (b)	1932	1937	1938 (a)	1938 (b)	1932	1937	1938 (a)	1938 (b)
Labourers —	Daily Paid																
Men —	Per Day	3/-	3/-	3/-	3/9	3/-	3/-	3/-	3/9	2/4	2/4	2/5	2/10	1/9	1/9	1/11	
Women —	" "	1/3	1/3	1/6	1/10½	1/6	1/6	1/6	1/10½	1/1	1/1	1/1	1/4	11d	1/-	11d	
Artisans —	Daily Paid																
Carpenters —	Per Day	7/-	7/-	7/-	7/-	7/-	7/-	7/-	7/-	5/6	6/-	6/4	6/7	4/7	5/-	5/2	
Masons —	" "	7/-	7/-	7/-	7/-	7/-	7/-	7/-	7/-	5/8	6/2	6/2	6/4	4/4	4/9	5/-	
Painters —	" "	7/-	7/-	7/-	7/-	7/-	7/-	7/-	7/-	5/5	6/-	6/-	6/1	4/5	4/7	4/1	
Mechanics —	" "	8/-	8/-	8/-	8/-	7/-	7/-	7/-	7/-	7/-	7/4	7/4		5/3	5/7	5/9	
Blacksmiths —	" "	8/-	8/4	7/6	7/6	7/-	7/-	7/6	7/6	6/-	6/6	6/3	7/-	4/9	5/-	5/-	

N.B. (a) Rates paid prior to the labour disturbances.
     (b) Rates paid subsequent to the labour disturbances.

As this table shows, during the seven years up to the beginning of 1938, that is before the disturbances of that year, male labourers in Kingston had received no wage increase. Their lower paid counterparts outside of Kingston had obtained daily increases of only 1d for those in the public service and 2d for those in private employment. Female labourers had got an increase of 4½d in Kingston, but nothing in the public service outside of Kingston. And although these women had by 1937 gained 1d in private employment, they had lost it again by the beginning of 1938. Artisans in Kingston, with the exception of black-smiths, had remained at the same rate over the seven year period, and the latter had lost ground to the extent of 6d in the public service though they had gained the same amount in private employment. Out-side of Kingston artisans had done slightly better, but their pay was still below that of their Kingston counterparts.

But low as these estimates of wages were, as set out in this memorandum submitted on behalf of the government, they were generally somewhat higher than those contained in other estimates submitted to the Royal Commission. A memorandum from one labour organisation stated:

> The general daily pay for the average worker on the Estates . . . at present, ranges from 1/6 to 2/6 for men, and for women 9d to 1/3. In very isolated cases since the past two months men have been paid 2/6 whilst women are paid 1/3.

The memorandum added that:

> in many cases, through our agitation and pressure . . . we have been able since the last 5 weeks to get a little increase on wages of workers on some Estates, but a great many of them still remain adamant in paying the same old starvation-slavish wages, whilst there are others who are paying their workers less than they had been paying up to three months ago.[32]

Whether this referred to a reduction of rates or a reduction of total weekly earnings was not specified.

Another memorandum, from the Organising Secretary of the same organisation in Lucea, Hanover, alleged that wage rates in that parish were below those of other parishes and that average earnings of the labouring men were 7/6 (75¢) per week and did not exceed 10/- ($1.00). The Public Works Department paid 2/6 (25¢) per day for men cutting roads, though 'in a very few cases . . . P.W. Dept. pays a maximum of three shillings [30¢] a day for 12 hour day.'[33]

Another labour organisation submitted evidence that banana loaders on the wharf were earning from 2/- (20¢) to 3/- (30¢) per day, adding that if the worker 'works in the day stretching into the night', he 'sometimes earns 3/-'.[34] A property owner in the parish of St. Mary, contradicting a statement made to his union by a labourer that his earnings totalled 6/- (60¢) per week, stated that the records showed that this man had earned an average total of 12/- ($1.20) for an average of three and a half to four days work per week.[35]

January 4th 1939, Wharf strike. Scene at Victoria Park Mtg.

Eight

The Events At Frome

1938 was to be a decisive year for the working class struggle in Jamaica. The events which provided the spark for the social conflagration occurred in Westmoreland, at the western end of the island. In the mid-1930s the English sugar refiners Tate & Lyle, in pursuance of a decision to go into cane sugar production in the West Indies, had bought up a number of sugar estates in Jamaica. In Westmoreland they had merged five estates into one and in March 1938 had commenced the building of a large new central sugar factory at Frome. The opportunities, or perceived opportunities, of employment there had attracted workers from all over the island.

On March 29, aware that dissatisfaction among the lowest paid manual workers was assuming island-wide proportions, the Governor announced the appointment of a Commission to enquire into rates of wages and conditions of employment of field and day labourers in receipt of not more than thirty shillings per week. The first session of this Commission was fixed for April 11.[36] Such a device might, in more normal times, have reduced unrest and bought a considerable amount of time, but on this occasion the tactic did not succeed. One of the reasons why this was so was the new expectations introduced by the publication of the plans of Tate & Lyle to develop sugar production in Jamaica.

The account of these plans in the *Daily Gleaner* of March 26, 1938 was most encouraging. Tate & Lyle, the announcement said, had recently acquired '16 or 17 sugar estates' and would be building a huge central factory and a narrow guage railway. Five hundred men, the story said, are now working on construction of the factory, and in another few months close to one thousand workers will be hammering and sawing, rivetting and digging. Modern cottages, a school and a church will be built. There will be daily transport for the labourers and 'these services will, of course, be free to labourers and their families'. Not surprisingly, given the generally low level of wages and the high level of unemployment, this news caused a considerable number of workers from all over the island to make their way to the parish of Westmoreland.

Matters came to a head at the end of April 1938. According to the official Report into the disturbances which followed:

> The main causes of complaints . . .were:
>
> (1)   that in consequence of an article alleged to have appeared in a newspaper to the effect that a large supply of labour was required . . . and that the Company was prepared to pay a minimum wage of a dollar [4/- or the equivalent of 40¢] a day, a great many labourers had flocked to Frome and then found that the report was untrue, that some could not get work, nor could they get back home
>
> (2)   inadequacy of the rates of pay
> (3)   delay in the payment of what was due
> (4)   the cutting of pay claimed to be due . . .

Nor were the workers willing to accept the Manager's explanation 'that this Company had not authorised the publication of any such statement and was not responsible for what appeared in the newspapers'. The management, according to the Report, 'attempted to improve the existing scale of pay and hours of work. When, however, this revised scale was communicated to the labourers they asserted that it did not substantially differ from the existing one, refused to accept it and the dissatisfaction was intensified.'[37]

According to this revised scale, general labourers were to receive 2/- (20¢) for a ten hour day (which included one hour off for lunch), with an extra 4d per hour for overtime. Mechanics, carpenters, electricians and masons were to get from 3/6 (35¢) per day upwards with 7d per hour for overtime and their apprentices a flat 1/6 (15¢) per day. Though these rates may have been in line with the rates paid in other parts of the island, they were obviously far below the workers' expectations. They therefore refused to accept them.

The *Daily Gleaner* of Monday, May 2, published the following account of how the strike started:

One thousand labourers, a large proportion of them engaged on the erection of a giant Central Sugar Factory at Frome Estate in Westmoreland, went on strike Friday. They are still out and state that they will only return to work when their demand — one Dollar [then 4/-] per day — is met by the West Indies Sugar Company ... Trouble started in the afternoon of Friday when some workmen received amounts which they claim involved a reduction of their pay by sums ranging from three pence to six pence per day.

The newspaper also reported the burning of canefields during the night, the arrival of local police from Savanna la Mar, Bluefields, Grange Hill and Little London, and the fact that a detachment of forty police from Kingston had been rushed to the scene.

Early next morning armed black policemen under the command of their white expatriate officers appeared at the building site in a provocative display of force. They were there to perform their principal colonial function as guardians of the property and profits of British investors. The representatives of Tate & Lyle were determined to stand firm against the strikers' demands and the colonial state was there to back them up to the full. But the strikers too were in a determined mood.

A newspaper reporter, representing the *Daily Gleaner,* sent in this report of the explosive situation:

Men and women armed with sticks and stones are milling about under the watchful eyes of armed police, shouting that they are willing to die on the spot unless their demands for a dollar a day wage are met right away by the management of the West Indies Sugar Coy. Ltd. The strikers to the number of about a thousand had been listening to passionate speeches by their fellows who have set themselves up to be leaders, and now they are running around arming themselves with anything they can lay their hands on — pieces of wood from three to five feet long, iron pipes, old iron axles and every conceiveable thing that can be used as a dangerous weapon.

'The old factory on the estate', he wrote, 'which up to Friday had been grinding canes, is entirely in the hands of the strikers'. Already stones were being thrown and he 'heard the crash of timber and glass shattered under the blows of stones and iron implements'. The reporter also showed a lively concern for his personal safety. 'The danger to life and limb was so great', he wrote, 'that it is impossible for me to hold my ground any longer and I am now moving out of the line of fire, for there is assuredly going to be shooting'.

As he left the scene he continued his story:

> Behind me, I hear rifle firing, followed by shrieks and cries ... I can see men on the ground. Some are motionless, others are staggering to and fro or crawling away on their hands and knees. The strike has culminated in stark tragedy. A few minutes later I hear that three are dead, eleven wounded and that the police are making many arrests.[38]

Four people were killed at Frome that day, three by police gunshot and one by a police bayonet. Nine of the wounded were admitted to hospital. Next day, discounting reports of larger numbers of wounded strikers in its new rival, the *Jamaica Standard,* the *Daily Gleaner* assured its readers that 'the known cases of persons suffering from wounds has not exceeded twenty-five, the arrests up to yesterday afternoon reached 96.'[39] But the wounded may indeed have been much more numerous. There was a widespread belief that anyone who sought medical treatment for injuries would be thereby identifying himself as a participant and inviting arrest.

Nine

Reactions To The Frome Events

Reports of the shootings at Frome had reached the capital on the same day. That night there was a large protest meeting at North Parade, after which St. William Grant led a march to the offices of the *Jamaica Standard* to make sure that the popular protest would be reported. Next day he led a demonstration of hundreds of workers through the streets of down-town Kingston. A press photographer who was covering the march was required to go with the demonstrators to a slum area in the west of the city known as 'the Dungle' (dunghill) to photograph the hovels in which destitute people were forced to live.[40]

The occurrences at Frome received full publicity in the press. The launching of a second big daily newspaper, the *Jamaica Standard,* shortly before these events had proved to be an important development. Anxious to boost its circulation the newspaper gave full publicity to what was happening and this made it impossible for the *Gleaner* to do otherwise than fully report the news. Everyone was therefore well informed about the labour unrest, strikes and demonstrations and the shootings of the strikers by the police. The whole island was in a state of considerable agitation.

Early on the morning of May 3, the day after these workers were killed by the police, Bustamante went to Frome where he met with the General Manager of the West Indies Sugar Company. Also present were the Inspector General and Deputy Inspector General of Police and other police officers. (In the 1930s police superintendents were called 'Inspectors'). After the meeting, Bustamante informed a *Gleaner* reporter that 'he was satisfied from records shown him that Tate & Lyle had spent and intended spending a great deal of money for the labourers and artisans employed by them insofar as providing excellent medical facilities and insuring sanitation were concerned'. He added that he had told the Manager 'that he did not think that the 2/- per diem

40

average . . . was adequate, nor that there would be peace at the factory so long as that scale of pay existed'. (The reporter actually recorded Bustamante as saying that this rate was inadequate for 'artisans', but presumably he meant 'labourers').

Bustamante praised the Company's plans for medical and dental services and the start made with the erection of cottages. According to the reporter, Bustamante 'left for the city . . . feeling satisfied that he had been able to accomplish something towards a better understanding between the management of Tate & Lyle's concern and the labouring element . . .'[41] Here once again we see Bustamante adopting a conciliatory attitude and endeavouring to play the role he, at that time, preferred — the role not of a trade union leader representing the workers but of a mediator between capital and labour.

The Governor, however, saw Bustamante's activities very differently. The Minutes of the Privy Council for May 7, 1938 recorded that:

> His Excellency consulted the Council in regard to the situation existing in the Corporate Area due to labour unrest and as to whether Mr. A. Bustamante, a labour leader, who had already made certain seditious utterances at public meetings and who had notified his intention of holding a mass meeting at the Kingston Race Course on Sunday the 8th May should be immediately arrested, with a view to the preservation of peace and good order.

The minutes recorded further that 'after full discussion, the Council advised that it would be inexpedient to effect the immediate arrest of Mr. Bustamante' but that 'his activities and the reaction thereto should . . . be closely watched and the question of his arrest reconsidered in the light of them'. The Governor accepted this advice.[42]

Hoping to snuff out the rebellious spirit of the workers which had surfaced at Frome, the Government rushed to trial a first batch of twenty-seven of the one hundred and nine workers arrested. They were brought before the Resident Magistrate at Savanna La Mar on May 13 and charged with 'riotous assembly'. At the same time the governor resorted to the time honoured device of setting up a Commission of Enquiry to enquire into the cause of these disorders.[43] In less than three weeks the Commission was in session at Frome ready to hear oral evidence. The West Indies Sugar Company retained N.W. Manley to represent them at the hearings — a retainer which Manley was later to find embarrassing.

41

Ten

Unrest Spreads While
Frome Trials Continue

The front page of the *Daily Gleaner* on Saturday May 14 was still
dominated by labour news. One report told of 'thousands of unemployed' who were marching 'from point to point seeking work'. The
appearance of Bustamante, the report continued, 'addressing a mass
meeting at North Parade at one o'clock in the day presented a spectacle
at once unusual and disturbing to the authorities'. Police with batons
were rushed to the scene but the crowd had already dispersed before
they arrived.

Another story told of a demand which had been made by the city's
waterfront workers for a reduction of the working day to eight hours.
Their present hourly rate was 9d and they were then working an eleven
hour day, with one paid hour off for lunch, for 8/3d (82½ᶜ). The workers
were proposing, said the report, that they should work eight hours for
6/- (60ᶜ) with overtime rates for any additional hours worked. As this
would have involved no increase in the basic hourly rate, the reporter
had probably got it wrong.

Yet another story was about the presence of three English communist seamen in Victoria Park where one of the men 'had climbed a
statue and declaimed against authority'. The *Gleaner* was worried that
they 'had gathered large groups of labourers around them and
delivered lectures embodying Communist ideals'. On another page it
was reported that labourers handling lumber at Leonard De Cordova's
wharf had been on strike from the previous day and were holding out
for restoration of 2d that had been cut from their hourly rate of 8d.
Workers handling lumber at Henderson's wharf, though still at work,
had made a similar demand.

On the following Monday the trial in Westmoreland was again the
subject of the *Gleaner's* main page one headline. On the second day a

serious discrepancy had appeared in the police evidence. One constable had claimed that the order to the police had been to fire 'overhead' and he 'heard no order to fire at the people'. But another constable said he had heard no such order. In reply to defence counsel he said that the only order he had heard was to fire. 'As a constable you understood from that you should fire at the mob to kill'?, asked counsel. 'Yes', the officer replied. Next day other witnesses confirmed that there had been no order to fire first above the heads of the crowd. Nor had the customary procedure of reading the Riot Act been observed.

The trial of the first batch of Frome workers charged for riotous assembly ended on May 19 with the conviction of fifteen and the imposition of sentences ranging from one year's imprisonment to thirty days. From the report in the *Daily Gleaner* of May 20 of what the Magistrate had to say when imposing the sentences, his determination to punish most severely those who could be identified as the 'ringleaders' of the strike was obvious.

On May 17 there was a demonstration in the Trench Town suburb of the city when a contractor, for whom workers were refusing to work because they alleged he had cheated them on a previous occasion, endeavoured to start work on his contract with the Kingston and St. Andrew Corporation (K.S.A.C.). Armed with sticks and pieces of iron, a large crowd prevented the enrolment of workers. They refused to allow the work to start unless the municipality would agree to eliminate the contractor and employ direct labour. The story got the *Gleaner's* main headline on May 18: 'Angry Unemployed Again Stop Work at Trench Town'. The use of the word 'unemployed' was not inappropriate. When the K.S.A.C. agreed to employ direct labour 250 men were enrolled to do the work, but the number estimated to have applied for the jobs was two thousand![44]

Eleven

The Waterfront Workers Strike

On May 19 the dispute on the Kingston waterfront came to a head.
When the 'Harboe Jensen' docked at the United Fruit Company Wharf,
to discharge a general cargo and take on a cargo of bananas, some two
hundred workers refused to handle the ship unless their hourly rates
were increased to 1/- (10^{c}) for longshoremen (dockside) and 1/3d (12½^{c})
for stevedores (on ship). The Company refused to increase the existing
rates and that night moved the ship to Port Antonio on the north coast,
where she was unloaded and loaded. The choice of Port Antonio was
deliberate. The waterfront workers there had been intimidated two
years earlier by the victimisation of their leader Lionel Lynch and
seventeen other members of the Jamaica Workers and Tradesmen's
Union, and they were not expected to give any further trouble.

The strike in Kingston, which had started at the United Fruit Company Wharf, spread to Grace Wharf, where the workers refused to
unload the 'Jamaica Planter' which had come in from England. On that
day, Friday May 20, a delegation of some thirty workers from No. 2
Railway Pier and Grace Wharf went to see Bustamante to ask him to
intervene. On the following day Bustamente met with the employers'
representatives, Messrs. Hislop and Molanphy, at the offices of the
United Fruit Company. He offered his services to both the employers
and employees as a mediator, but his offer was rejected by the
employers. Informing a representative of the *Gleaner* of the results of
the meeting, Bustamante said that the employers were 'unwilling to
grant any concessions to the workmen while on strike. Their only words
were to the affect that the labourers must return to work, then elect a
deputation to discuss the differences with them'.[45]

The same day, May 21, Bustamante had a meeting with R.F.
Williams of the Jamaica Banana Producers Association and E.C.

Joysey of the Jamaica Fruit and Shipping Company, whose ship, the 'Jamaica Planter', was tied up by the strike at Grace Wharf. Afterwards Bustamante complained that he had been 'snubbed' and treated with discourtesy. In reply the Company denied discourtesy, informing the *Gleaner* reporter that 'Mr. Bustamante, on being asked whether he officially represented the men, stated that he did not, but that he was acting in a friendly manner as a go-between, between employer and employee'. Mr. Williams said further: 'that a go-between was really unnecessary as the management had always been ready and was still ready to discuss labour conditions with its employees of every class[46] Once again, Bustamante had sought to intervene, not as a labour leader but as an impartial mediator seeking a reconciliation between the workers and their employers.

Deeply offended, Bustamante referred the matter to the workers. This is how I recorded these developments in a letter written soon after the event.[47]

> By Sunday the strike had spread to every wharf in Kingston. The men demanded 1/- per hour and overtime at 2/- per hour. Bustamante, at gigantic meeting on Sunday morning gave the people two alternatives:
>
> (a)   Strike now
>
> (b)   Let me first negotiate, and if I don't get your demands for you, strike tomorrow.
>
> They selected the former. The United Fruit Company offered the sailors on board the 'Veragua' 5/- [50¢] per hour to unload the ship but they refused, and four of them addressed the men, advising them to hold out. They collected $32.25 on board and turned it over to Bustamante to help with food.

These American seamen had received a telegram from the National Maritime Union urging them to support the strike. I learned later that the General Secretary of their union was a Jamaican seaman who had been away for nearly twenty years. His name, Ferdinand Smith, was later to become significant in Jamaica when he returned home in the 1950s.

Meanwhile the situation was by no means calm at the western end of the island. The trial of a second batch of thirty-one of the prisoners in custody in Westmoreland, charged with riotous assembly at Frome on May 2, had commenced on Friday May 20. On Sunday May 22 the lightermen loading sugar at Montego Bay had come out on strike. Everywhere there were signs of increasing tension.

Aware of the rising mood of determination among the workers, our Marxist group had been earnestly discussing the need to strengthen the J.W.T.U. in the rural areas, to organise other unions along industrial lines in the urban areas and to bring all the trade unions together in a federation of labour. We had also recognized the necessity for a working class newspaper and Buchanan had been making the necessary arrangements for this with Stennet Kerr Coombs, the owner of a small job-printery. The first issue of the *Jamaica Labour Weekly,* edited by Buchanan and printed by Coombs, was published on 14 May 1938 — a single sheet printed on both sides. By the second issue it had grown to four pages, the size at which it remained.

Kingston Workers' march 1938.

Twelve

Kingston On May 23

But let us return to the developments which were taking place on the Kingston waterfront. I recorded these events in my letter of June 1 referred to above. This is how that letter continued:

> On Monday began the general tie-up. The dockmen early in the morning were addressed by Bustamante. Here is an extract from his speech:
>
> 'These companies will have to meet us with material results. Just because the companies are rich they tell you until you go back to work they will not tell you whether or not they will do anything for you. Until they give in I shall tie up the wharves. I am going to tie up every store in King Street. The time when these managers could tell you they will not do anything until you return to work is past and gone. The stores that are paying their clerks 9/- per week are going to close. I did not start the strike. I was merely acting as a mediator, but we will stay out, and those ships will not be loaded. And if those companies are not more reasonable, I am going to tie up every port in the Island'.

By the morning of Monday May 23, Bustamante was firmly committed to siding with the striking waterfront workers. But what of the poorly paid shop assistants whom he had mentioned tangentally during his speech? Some of them at least were members of a union, the Jamaica United Clerks Association. How did they react to Bustamante's rhetoric? In the same letter I commented on their reaction:

> The shops on King Street were certainly closed, but by dockmen and their sympathisers, not by the shop assistants working for 9/- and 8/- [per week]. These were to be observed clapping their hands from the tops of the buildings, as police drove a small band of strikers from lower King Street. The shop assistants' union is under the reactionary leadership of one E.E.A. Campbell, Barrister-at-Law, who at the moment appears to be working hard to remove all thought of a strike from their minds. They are, of course, far too snobbish to sympathise with ordinary labour.

May 23 was the day on which the widespread feelings of discontent among the manual workers erupted in strikes throughout the capital. As the street cleaners too had been on strike from the previous day, no garbage had been removed and the streets had not been swept. They were demanding an increase in their pay of 3/- and 4/- per day to a minimum of thirty shillings per week, plus overtime for work on Sundays and public holidays. They also demanded rain cloaks and water boots for use in wet weather.[48]

I went to office as usual that morning but by 8.30 a.m. it was obvious that everything was in turmoil and no work was likely to be done. I then went to see what was happening on the streets and during that day and until about 9 o'clock in the evening, covered as much of the city as possible on foot. These extracts from the account I wrote, on the following day, of what I had seen will help to fill in the picture:

> Bands of workers closed all shops throughout the city. Was standing at door of Scotland's when small body of about twelve young men came up from Harbour Street and ordered his assistants to close the shutters. One shutter was closed and then about nine or ten police charged. The band scattered, and one man got hit over the head with a truncheon . . .
>
> Outside Jamaica Fruit Bustamante and Grant were holding a meeting. There was a large crowd completely blocking the street. There was a detachment of police east of the meeting . . . Bustamante finished his address and he and Grant moved east along Harbour Street. Some of the crowd started to follow. Then the police executed an absolutely unprovocated [sic] charge with battons, laying into men, old men and women indiscriminately . . .
>
> At 11.30 . . . I went to Public Opinion to try and persuade them to issue a pamphlet to the shop assistants whom I had noticed were clapping from the top of the King Street buildings when the small band earlier mentioned was driven off from Scotland's . . .
>
> . . . Proceeded up King Street to South Parade where Bustamante, Grant and others were holding a meeting from the statue. Bustamante told everyone to go home . . . Bustamante tried to get the people to sing 'God Save the King', but very few obliged, and the meeting ended. The crowd however did not disperse . . .
>
> It was now about 12 a.m. [sic]. There was a body of police . . . about 60 to 80 . . . They spread across the road and advanced in a solid line mercilessly wielding their batons. They went right across clearing the Parade. I saw a ragged, bare-footed woman beaten till she fell to the ground, and the policeman stood over her and struck her across the back of the neck and shoulders as she lay there . . . Another man was beaten badly and I saw him being escorted to

safety between Bustamante and Grant. (The Police did not touch them) . . .

In the wake of the police came four (or five) little army trucks manned by soldiers in tin helmets . . . The police then formed up and systematically cleared the park working from south to north. As I with the rest was driven towards the north of the park, I saw stationed there some of the little army trucks manned by soldiers. Most of the soldiers in the trucks had rifles. I . . . could not see whether they had any other guns in the trucks.

Bustamante and Grant were . . . walking side by side . . . They . . . walked down the side of the park on East Parade . . . A crowd began to follow but a body of police drove them back with batons. My companion and I were . . . turned back by the police . . . One old man resented their attitude and stood his ground. This was the only occasion on which I saw a policeman use the slightest consideration, and he . . . merely pushed and swore at him.

We . . . went west along North Street to the Hospital as far as we could go. There was a guard of soldiers and police. The . . . Laboratory was in a sorry state. Every window was broken, and some sheets of a zinc fence at the rear had been torn out. Upon enquiring we learned that Dr. Evans . . . had attempted to drive through and knocked down three women. Thereupon the strikers had cut up rough and he had drawn a gun and shot someone. He had escaped into the laboratory and the mob had besieged the place . . . The police and soldiers had arrived and driven the people off . . .[49]

From earlier in the day the tram operators had stopped work. The drivers and conductors of the motor buses had begun to come out on strike too. The official Report to the Legislative Council records that in Kingston:

By 11 a.m. all transport services (tram and bus) had ceased to operate, practically all labour had been suspended and business was at a complete stand still. Hostility to the police had become more marked and they were frequently stoned.[50]

Early that afternoon I joined a group of bus drivers who had just sighted a Hope Gardens bus going up Upper King Street. They set off in pursuit and stopped it. The driver offered no resistance and agreed to take it back to the garage. During all this excitement there had been a scuffle between two women food vendors and the pan of patties of one of them had capsized. Young bystanders then grabbed some of the patties and made off with them. What happened next I recorded in my account:

. . . one of the busmen summoned his fellows round him and held a short conference. We then returned to the site of the scuffle, and someone was sent to call the woman who had fled. The leader got up on a box, told his hearers that there must be no looting of that kind, took a collection in his hat, and paid the woman for patties, in the upsetting and seizing of which the busmen had had absolutely no part. Then the march was on again: Into the West to stop the country buses before they pulled out at three o'clock.[51]

As the day wore on barricades were erected across many roads and streets. Making my way northwards on foot in the afternoon I passed a barricade at Torrington Bridge and another on the Old Hope Road above Babbins Church. Even where there were no barricades, motorists could make only slow progress because of obstacles which littered the roads. 'Slipe Road', I noted 'was a mass of debris of all sorts, stones, rocks, an old motor car chassis, the body, an old engine, garbage cans, and God knows what else'.

I noted a number of incidents in which police and soldiers attempted to clear people from the streets, sometimes with batons, sometimes with bullets. There were also several instances of people fighting back, sometimes with stones and sticks.

According to the official Report:

> There were minor clashes between the Police and the populace throughout the day . . . In Kingston from 6 p.m. on the Monday to 6 a.m. on the Tuesday morning the city was patrolled by units of Police, Local Forces and Special Constables. They were frequently attacked by mobs concealed in dark lanes and alleys, which occasionally fired shots but in the main relied on stones.

The Report stated further:

> a number of men were injured during the night some seriously, but none by bullets. The work of the patrols was hampered by the destruction of the street lamps.

It is also noted that three Chinese groceries were set on fire and that 'By 2.30 a.m. the city was quiet'.[52] As might be expected, this official version makes much of the part played by 'hooligans' and even 'habitual criminals'.

There had also been indications on May 23 that the popular unrest was beginning to spread to other parts of the island. According to the official report, labourers went on strike for higher wages in Spanish Town, thirteen miles from Kingston, and crowds there were reported to

51

be on the march. Some twelve miles further to the west, the Report continued, 'something similar took place in Old Harbour Town area'. A short strike had taken place on a wharf at Montego Bay and strikes were also reported on Llandovery and Drax Hall estates in St. Ann.[53]

On this day the Government put in motion the enrolment of persons described as 'Special Constables', a process which continued for several weeks. Initially the persons recruited were mostly light complexioned members of the upper and middle classes. With guns in their hands these people could be relied upon to enter into the task of subduing the rebellious black masses with enthusiasm. The creation of this force was particularly ominous. Many of the workers who were killed and wounded or otherwise physically maltreated during May and June were the victims of this armed auxiliary force. However, as the weeks went by and these upper and middle class recruits returned to their administrative and office jobs, the social composition of the Special Constabulary began to change. The places of the original recruits were taken by black men with a more mercenary motivation. From an initial enrolment of two hundred at the Central Police Station in Kingston on May 23,[54] their number eventually rose to several thousand.

Thirteen

May 24 — Arrest of Bustamante And Grant

May 24 was a public holiday, the old 'Empire Day', and normally there would have been no newspapers. But such was the state of excitement on that day that the Gleaner Company brought out two special issues which, as they proudly announced next day, were circulated 'all over the island'.

That day, in the words of the official Report on the disturbances: 'Crowds began to gather in the capital early in the morning and police and military were engaged throughout the day in breaking them up . . . Military trucks patrolled the streets at frequent intervals'. Bustamante and Grant were prevented from addressing a crowd on the Spanish Town Road.[55]

At about 9.15 a.m. a mobile party of police encountered a crowd at the corner of Princess and Heywood Streets in Kingston which, according to the official Report, 'refused to disperse and began to stone the Police'. The Report alleged that the police fired twelve rounds 'at the ground between them and mob'. When the firing ceased a woman who had been at an upstairs window of No. 137 Princess Street had been fatally wounded. How had this happened? According to the official Report, her death was in consequence of being hit by a police bullet which had 'ricoched' off the pavement.

Eye witnesses gave a very different account of the incident. One such witness said: 'The strikers had arrived in a large body and a patrol of police rushed to the scene'. The police had 'fired at the crowd for they had now started throwing stones at the military might. A tall policeman with a rifle and a man in plain clothes with a revolver thought the stones had come from No. 137, so they fired up into the house. Seven shots . . . were fired into the house'. Reporting this, the *Gleaner* confirmed that 'many holes were seen by the reporter, in the windows, on the walls and in the ceiling'.[56]

At about 10 a.m. 'police and special constables opened fire in Matthews Lane, killing two members of one family and injuring a third'. Dead were a woman and her nine year old son. Her six year old child, seriously wounded, was taken to the public hospital. A *Gleaner* reporter who arrived shortly afterwards 'found a scene of indescribable confusion. The remaining members of the unfortunate family were screaming hysterically while police clubbed men and women who assembled in the lane'.[57]

Meanwhile at about the same hour, Bustamante and Grant had gone to the Fire Brigade headquarters 'followed by a mob', to quote the official Report, and 'with the object of inducing or forcing the Fire Brigade to strike'. The Governor had, in the meantime, decided to have them arrested and the police caught up with them there and took them into custody. A magistrate remanded them in custody for a week.[58]

Whatever Bustamante's intentions may have been, it is known that the men of the Fire Brigade had made demands for wage increases which had not been met. In view of the reputation as a friend of the workers that Bustamante had acquired, it is not surprising that the firemen should have sought his intervention. However, it does not appear that their decision to strike, if their demands were not met, was made until after their attempt to enlist Bustamante's support had been frustrated. When their intention became known, there was consternation in official circles.

Fourteen

N.W. Manley's Intervention

On May 23 Norman Manley had been at Frome where he was representing the West Indies Sugar Company at the Commission of Enquiry into the events of May 2nd. He returned to Kingston on receipt of a telegram which read, according to his diary: 'Riot — come back'. He does not say who sent the telegram but it was probably from his wife Edna. We can take up the story from this point by further reference to Manley's 'diary' (a record made on June 11, 1938 which he described as 'a note on facts before I forget them') and his subsequently written memoirs:

> *Monday, May 23rd* arrived Kingston from Frome in answer to 2 telegrams. Number 2 says 'Deny remour', Number 1 — 'Riot — come back'. I come late and am abused [he does not say by whom]. Next day perambulate.[59]

What did Manley see on his 'perambulations' around the city on May 24. This he recalled in his memoirs:

> ... knots of silent sullen people waiting in ugly frame of mind. I did not at all like what I saw. Then I heard there was trouble at the fire Brigade and set off to go there when I heard that they were to strike that afternoon and that Bustamante had gone there to address them when he and his faithful friend of those days, St. William Grant, had been arrested ... Near the Fire Brigade I saw a few people I knew very well and paused to talk when Audley Morais [a wealthy businessman] rushed up and besought me, almost with tears in his eyes, to go and talk with the men in the Fire Brigade for God knows what would happen if they did go on strike.

Manley recalled further:

> eventually I went and met nearly all the men actually at Brigade H.Q. I heard all sorts of complaints and spoke to the men, promising to go and see the Mayor, Dr. Anderson and K.S.A.C. officials

and to take up the matter till I got a final settlement. My intervention was welcomed by the men who knew me well, at least by name,
and I dashed off to see the Mayor and set up a conference with the
Brigade for the next day. I saw nothing that could not be cleared up
in one conference and indeed so it turned out.[60]

News of the arrest of Bustamante and Grant on May 24 had spread
like wild fire and there were a number of clashes between strikers and
the police and soldiers all over the corporate area. Next day the arrest
was reported in the newspapers and was known all over the island. Over
the next few days what had been developing into a general strike in the
capital began to assume island-wide proportions. To the demands for
wage increases that were everywhere being made there was now added
a demand for the release of Bustamante.

At 10 p.m. on the night of May 24, a special court was assembled at
the Central Police Station, presided over by the principal stipendiary
magistrate of the Criminal Division. An application for bail was made
by J.A.G. Smith, K.C. (the member of the Legislative Council for
Clarendon) instructed by solicitor Ross Livingston. Acting Crown Prosecutor, T.H. Mayers, one of the many official sent out from England by
the Colonial Office in those days to serve in the colonies, opposed the
application on behalf of the Government. Giving evidence for the
Crown, Police Inspector W.A. Orrett stated that 'even though Mr. Bustamante and Mr. Grant might be willing to stand trial, the crowd would
not allow them to and thus the ends of justice may be frustrated'. Bail
was refused.[61]

That night, according to Manley's diary, he tried unsuccessfully to
persuade the Governor 'to release Bustamante on his assurance he
would not act to public mischief'. Manley recorded that he 'felt a martyr
was being made'. In his subsequently written memoirs he recalled that
he had been 'deeply persuaded ... that with Bustamante arrested and
all workers in the Corporate Area on strike we were in for a serious time
and that violence, disorder and bloodshed would be the final
result.'

Fifteen

Manley Offers To Serve Labour

Despite the Governor's refusal to release Bustamante, Manley decided to intervene in the waterfront dispute to try to bring about a settlement and return to work. In his diary record of his meeting with the Governor on the Tuesday May 24, he noted:

> I suggest I act and he begs me to — I say I will think. That night I decide and send for reporters and offer service.

Manley's decision was featured on the front pages of the newspapers. The *Daily Gleaner* of May 25 carried the story:

> Realising the need for leadership, Mr. N.W. Manley K.C. has come out to represent the cause of the labourers with a view to having their grievances remedied and so has placed his services at the disposal of the working classes to present their cases to the employers and the authorities. Interviewed last night Mr. Manley stated that the events that have happened since Sunday have proved how necessary it is today that the people of the country should have good leadership and good advice in putting forward their grievances and making their demands.

Manley expressed the view that all should 'deplore what happened on Monday'; that 'creating complete confusion and disorder, endangering innocent people's lives, destroying property and compelling Government to call out armed forces' was only 'putting the clock to progress backward'. He was, he said, 'convinced that Government is anxious that the people should have an opportunity of making representations . . . and that one of the greatest difficulties in the way of any desire on the part of Government to assist in these troubles is the difficulty of finding persons who are willing to assist the labouring classes and putting forward their grievances'.

For these reasons, said Manley, 'I feel that at this stage of affairs anybody who can assist . . . and who has the interest of the country at heart, should do what he can to help, and I wish to state . . . that if any labour group . . . concerned in this strike will accept my services in investigating their grievances and in acting for them by advising them and by leading their deputations in making representations to employer interests or to the Governor himself or to the Labour Commission which has been appointed. I pledge myself to serve their interests fairly and properly and to give every assistance to see that reasonable and fair demands are met . . .'

Finally, said the great man: 'It is hoped that when the present troubles are over, some group of responsible people will recognise the necessity for organising proper trade unions in this country'. 'It has been rumoured', he concluded, 'that I have advised some of the activities of the past few days. It is sufficient to say that nobody who knows me could possibly believe that I could think that Jamaica's interests would be served by letting loose the irresponsible pandemonium of the past two days'.[62]

The Governor, of course, was delighted at Manley's intervention. Manley recorded in his diary:

> Next day H.E. phones at 9 and says he likes notice but it says nothing about 'return to work first' — I say I must act fully for labour and with a free hand.

But if the failure on Manley's part to say that there must be a return to work disappointed the Governor, his failure to say publicly what he had told the Governor privately — that there would be no industrial peace until Bustamante and Grant were released — was a dissapointment to the workers.

Tuesday May 24th Busta arrested, scene outside Sutton St. gaol.

Sixteen

Workers Stand Firm — Unrest Spreads

Not surprisingly, unrest had not subsided and the newspapers continued to report strikes, demonstrations and clashes between strikers and the armed forces. On May 24 the 'Lady Rodney' was unable to unload its cargo from Montreal, though it did succeed in taking on some bananas on the north coast before returning to Canada. Jamaican soldiers of the Kingston Infantry Volunteers were sent to disperse a large crowd on Hanover Street and a youth in the front of the crowd was bayonetted through the leg. Two girls and a man received gun-shot wounds on North Street from a mobile military patrol.

Bus operators of the Magnet Bus Company went on strike, as did road workers at Glengoffe in St. Mary. In Spanish Town a patrol of police and Special Constables met retaliation with stones when it dispersed a crowd on Salt Lane and a constable received a shoulder injury from a shot fired from a revolver. This, however, was unusual as strikers who could have obtained fire arms would have been very few indeed.[63]

There were signs from all over the country on May 25 that labour unrest was increasing. The *Gleaner* reported that strikers had been demonstrating at Highgate in St. Mary and Bog Walk in St. Catherine. At Caymanas Estate six workers were shot and wounded by Special Constables under the command of the estate manager, P.A. Bovell, three of them seriously enough to be admitted at the Spanish Town Hospital. The manager denied that the company's employees were on strike, alleging that the people who were preventing work were 'a gang of hooligans' whom he had found 'in control of the whole estate'. 'I then got together my Special Constables', he said ' . . . read the Riot Act and then ordered my Special Constables to clear them out'.[64]

A significant development on May 25 was the refusal of the wharf workers at Bowden and Port Morant in St. Thomas, unlike those at

Port Antonio and certain other north coast ports, to load bananas. This was the beginning of a movement in the out-ports to join the strike. Kingston shop assistants, in stores on West Queen Street, Princess Street and Beckford Street, and the subordinate staff at the Kingston Public and Jubilee hospitals also came out on strike. Meanwhile, tram and bus operators employed by the Jamaica Public Service Company decided to continue their strike, when the manager refused to continue negotiations unless work was resumed. But later, as it was believed that the manager would receive authority to grant increases from the parent company in Canada, the *Gleaner* reported that a return to work was expected on the following morning.

Seventeen

Bustamante Again Refused Bail

A development on May 25 which was to have important repercussions was the government's continuing opposition to the granting of bail for Bustamante and Grant. The application for bail came before a resident magistrate at the Kingston Criminal Court at mid-day. The accused were brought across the road from the Central Police Station under heavy police escort after the crowd that had begun to assemble earlier in the day had been dispersed by a massive show of armed force.

The government was again represented by Acting Crown Prosecutor Mayers. There had been some doubt up to this point as to exactly what the charges were and the Magistrate read them out. Bustamante was charged on two counts of sedition, allegedly uttered in a speech made on May 4, after his return to Kingston. He was also charged with inciting a large crowd to assemble unlawfully on May 24 and obstructing Police Inspector W.A. Orrett in the execution of his duty. Grant was charged with refusing to obey an order and inciting people to assemble unlawfully. Neither accused was asked to state what his plea would be to the charges.[65]

The trick of scaring people away from participation in progressive activities by alleging that the particular activity is part of a 'communist' plan to cause disruption, is an old one which, everywhere in the capitalist dominated world, is used to discourage change. Distortions of what communists stand for are followed by misrepresentations of what they are trying to achieve by organising the workers. Where communist influence is small or non existent it is exaggerated or invented. It is therefore not surprising that in May 1938 suggestions should have begun to appear in the press that communists were at work creating strife and disorder in Jamaica.

Here is a typical item of this kind which appeared in the *Daily Gleaner* on May 14. 'Communism Here! Suspicion is growing . . . that Communist money is being spent in Jamaica. The apparent restiveness of labour in various sections of the island simultaneously, is regarded as more than mere coincidence, or the result of economic pressure'. On May 23 the *Gleaner* followed this with a report that 'certain gentlemen' in Montego Bay believed that 'certain persons receiving emoluments from the Communist Party of Cuba were responsible for the recent Frome riot'. A prominent Kingston merchant and wharf owner, Frank E. Lyons, who happened to be one of Jamaica's best known radio hams, was busy telling everyone he met that he had heard a broadcast from Moscow referring to 'the work Comrade Bustamante is doing in Jamaica'.

When the application for bail for Bustamante was being heard in Court on May 25, prosecutor Mayers hinted at organisational connections in a manner designed to suggest that Bustamante might be an agent for foreign communists. Replying, Bustamante's solicitor 'contradicted the submission by Mr. Mayers that Bustamante might be connected with any organisation'. The prosecutor then made a tactical retreat, which did not however completely purge his submission of its impropriety. The Crown, he said, 'was neutral on the point'.

Eighteen

Manley Negotiates With Employers

On May 25 an *Emergency Powers Law* was rushed through all its stages in the Legislative Council and the Governor declared a state of emergency. Despite this Manley, who had been approached on behalf of the waterfront workers, had proceeded to open negotiations with the shippers on their behalf. His diary disclosed two conflicting points of view among the employers. He recorded that C.E. Johnson, (a Director of Kingston Wharves Ltd and an important person on the shipping side of the Jamaica Banana Producers Association) 'sees that all wages must go up' and is for reconciliation. On the other hand R.F. Williams (a big planter and Director of the J.B.P.A.) 'doesn't like what he sees and is for [using] force' [against the workers]. But added Manley 'C.E. Johnson [is] very helpful — two [pence per hour] on day work agreed'.

May 25 was a particularly busy day for Manley. Many groups of workers, on strike in different industries and occupations, had decided to take advantage of his offer to negotiate on their behalf and volunteers were at work in his chambers recording their demands and arranging appointments for meetings with employers. The latter, scared out of their wits by the spontaneous upsurge that had occurred, were only too anxious to negotiate settlements. But the strike of longshoremen and stevedores on the Kingston waterfront had obviously become the key to the situation. The *Gleaner* of May 26 carried the following statement from Norman Manley addressed to the water-front workers:

> I have been in conference with wharf-owners and shipping agents and representatives of the Government all day yesterday and I have put forward the case of the ship and wharf labourers, together with Mr. E.E.A. Campbell, who has been associated with me and is giving every assistance. At this stage I will only announce that the

deliberations have resulted in definite proposals which I wish to place before you when I will give you my advice and say what I recommend.

The statement then went on to give details of a meeting of all waterfront workers which was to take place on the following morning at No. 1 Railway Pier, and to explain the elaborate arrangements made with the shippers to ensure that all but waterfront workers would be excluded. Manley appealed to 'genuine' waterfront workers 'to help see that idlers who have no concern in the business do not come to interfere with the proceedings'.

Explaining how busy he had been to other groups of workers whom he had not had time to see, Manley assured them that he was willing to meet them all. He therefore appealed to them to be patient and 'not to take advantage of the situation to stir up disorder, and not to interrupt services which are essential to the well being of the country'.[66]

Nineteen

No Work Till Bustamante Is Free

So Manley had negotiated an increase with the employers on the Kingston waterfront, who were ready to concede a part of what the workers were demanding. But what did the workers have to say? Manley recorded this in his diary:

> W.A. Williams[67] for labour says men won't budge. I go to Malabre's Wharf and talk to a huge crowd in the street. I get a patient hearing. We are to meet *en masse* next morning [May 26].

That afternoon Buchanan and I went to see Manley on behalf of our Marxist group. We tried to persuade him that it would be a betrayal of the workers' cause to advise them to return to work while Bustamante and Grant were still in prison. It appears that we weren't very tactful and our reception was not very friendly. Manley recorded this meeting in his diary as follows:

> *Wednesday afternoon* saw Hart and H.C. Buchanan — the latter full of venom, the former *bitter re* Dock Strike. I speak bluntly.

Convinced of the danger that Manley would persuade the workers to go back to work, Buchanan acted swiftly and decisively, going straight to the printery to prepare a leaflet. He didn't submit what he proposed to do to the group. The accusation in the leaflet was harsh and a somewhat unfair over-simplification. Had it been submitted to the group, we would certainly have wanted to modify the language, thereby possibly lessening its impact. No doubt that was why we were not consulted. By that evening and early next morning hundreds of copies of the leaflet were being distributed on the waterfront. It read:

MANLEY AND CAMPBELL CANNOT BE TRUSTED
TOOLS OF THE CAPITALISTS
AWAY WITH THEM
SUPPORT BUSTAMANTE AND GRANT

66

This leaflet, which was reproduced in the next issue of the *Jamaica Labour Weekly*,[68] helped to stiffen the resolve of the workers not to go back to work until Bustamante and Grant were released. They were in such a militant mood, however, that that might have been their decision even without the leaflet. At the mass meeting on the following day they left Manley in no doubt as to their intentions. Manley recorded the event in his diary:

> *Wednesday night* Buchanan issues pamphlet 'Don't trust'. I am warned not to go to docks.

> *Thursday* mass meeting at docks. I speak and offer rejected. I quarrel with W.A. Williams who told them reject, but he sticks to his guns.

In the words of the official report:

> Bustamante and Grant being in custody and bail having been refused, Mr. N.W. Manley, KC, an outstanding member of the Jamaica Bar, and a former Rhodes Scholar, came forward and offered himself as mediator between the wharf strikers and the shipping companies. He succeeded in gaining concessions from the latter but the strikers refused to resume work until Bustamante and Grant had been released on bail.[69]

So Manley's advice to the workers to return to work on the basis of wage increases negotiated by him, whilst the imprisonment of Bustamante and Grant continued, had been rejected. There was no eye-witness report of the meeting at which this had taken place in the next morning's newspapers, as the press had been excluded. But newspaper reporters had got the gist of the matters discussed from the workers as they came out of the wharf. The *Gleaner* of May 27 carried two stories concerning the matter. A front page item reported that after the meeting truck loads of workers had emerged chanting 'No work, no work', and 'We don't want 1/- an hour. We want Bustamante'. A fuller report on an inside page stated:

> An offer was put forward by Mr. Manley on behalf of the Shipping Companies of a raise of 2d per hour for wharf labourers bringing it up to 10d for work on the wharf and 11d for work on the ship, but the labourers declined the offer, standing out for 1/- [10¢] per hour and 2/- [20¢] per hour overtime, stipulating in addition that the first condition of return to work must be the release of Bustamante and Grant.[70]

Twenty

Workers Close Down Spanish Town

May 26 was a day on which the workers provided fresh evidence of their militant determination to win wage increases and more job opportunities and also to secure the release of Bustamante and Grant. That day and during the night the workers took over the streets of Spanish Town and brought all work to a halt, just as they had done two days previously in the capital. *Gleaner* reports of the situation suggested that the shootings of workers by the Special Constables at Caymanas on the previous day had been an important cause of their anger and resentment.

Newspaper reports indicated that during the day the strikers had displayed a high degree of organisation in bringing all work to a halt. 'The mob organised itself and sent out riders on bicycles to different vital centres to order that work be stopped. If these scouts were not obeyed, the mob was summoned to enforce the order. Thus they closed shops of all alien [Chinese and Syrian] traders, stopped the street cleaners from continuing work (these had just resumed after getting an increase of pay following their strike) and even tried to close down the whole water undertaking of the town [which had an armed guard]'. Workers also visited the hospital, where they demanded that work should stop 'as they said the nurses were underpaid and over worked'. But when the doctor in charge 'told them he would see that nurses' conditions were improved', they agreed to allow them to continue working.

Police and military reinforcements were rushed over from Kingston and Special Constables, some reportedly using their own guns, were also brought into action. But, according to the *Gleaner* report, the events that night saw 'every inch of ground contested'. The armed forces fired on the demonstrators and several were wounded. But 'the mob replied with heavy missiles and fought every inch of the way'. Some policemen and Special Constables were injured.[71] The newspapers also reported new strikes at Richmond in St. Mary, May Pen in Clarendon, Bog Walk in St.Catherine and Montego Bay and strikes in Kingston at the tobacco station on the Spanish Town Road, at the Machado Tobacco Company at Victoria Avenue and at the Jamaica Shoe Factory on Harbour Street.

Soon after the strike started Aggie Bernard and her sister, two working class women in West Kingston, started cooking free meals for strikers at the waterfront who had no money to buy food. It was a magnificent initiative, but being very poor themselves they had to appeal to others to assist. There was a good response, Edna Manley the wife of Norman Manley being one of the earliest financial contributors. With her assistance and that of others the service had, by May 27, been expanded to provide one thousand five hundred strikers with a midday meal. The response extended to the rural areas and at the waterfront workers' meeting on that morning the donation of two truck-loads of bananas and coconuts was announced. On May 28 a notice appeared in the newspapers which read:

> Longshoremen Fund. Longshoremen request that no money be collected on the street by anyone; but if any persons are in sympathy with the strikers and wish to contribute anything, money may be sent to Mrs. N.W. Manley, 21 Duke Street, either by post or hand.[72]

Twenty-One

Plans For a Waterfront Workers Union

The tremendous upsurge of working class militancy in May 1938 was interpreted by our Marxist group as clear evidence that the majority of the workers would now respond to the call to advance from unorganised to organised struggle. We saw the possibility of organising trade unions on a much wider scale than had been achieved up to that point and on or about May 24 I had sent a cable to O'Meally and Domingo in New York asking them to contact the Congress of Industrial Organisations, the more progressive of the two U.S. trade union centres, for literature on the organisation of industrial trade unions.[73]

On May 26 an emergency conference was convened by the National Reform Association at which a delegation of strikers from the Kingston waterfront led by W.A. Williams was present. The purpose of the meeting was to discuss a proposal from N.R.A. Secretary, Ken Hill, for the formation of a waterfront workers trade union. Also present at the meeting was Ross Livingston, Bustamante's solicitor, who informed the workers' representatives that the proposal had the approval of Bustamante. The workers' representatives agreed to the proposal on the understanding 'that on the formation of the union their leader, Mr. Alexander Bustamante, shall be appointed President'. The *Gleaner* on May 27 reported that 'the following letter was issued as a result of the conference'.[74]

26 May 1938

W.A. Williams, Esq.

Dear Sir,

I suggest the dock men form themselves into a trade union and appoint Mr. Bustamante as President. In this way there will be a legal and organized body ready to hand to negotiate with wharf owners and shipping companies and Government . . .

This suggestion is put forward by the Council of the National Reform Association and has been placed before Mr. Bustamante and has been approved by him.

Yours faithfully,

R.C. Livingston

This was a very important and interesting development. It marked the turning point at which Bustamante was compelled, by circumstances, to abandon his chosen role as an impartial public spirited mediator between capital and labour and accept the fact that he had become a labour leader. He had been propelled into this role by the irresistible combination of the intransigence of the employers, the high handedness of the Government and the militancy of the workers.

Twenty-Two

Government Hopes Strikes Will Collapse

But although the die had been cast, the establishment was not yet ready to accept the inevitability of the situation. Strengthened by the arrival on the morning of May 26 of the warship HMS 'Ajax', hastily summoned from the Bermuda naval station, the Governor was still intent on a course of intimidation. He appears to have hoped that a massive show of force and the continued imprisonment of Bustamante would bring about a collapse of the strike. When another application was made for bail by barrister Smith on May 26, this time to one of the English judges of the High Court, the Government again opposed it and the application was again refused. That day, according to the official report of the disturbances:

> At a conference attended by naval, military and police representatives, measures were discussed for protecting willing labour in working the wharves if it became necessary to import essential food supplies. It was agreed that in this event the Royal Navy should protect the wharves while the Army would continue to find the mobile reserves and truck patrols. The Royal Navy might, however, be asked to take over all or part of these latter duties to relieve police and troops for duty outside Kingston if the situation became worse in the country.[75]

What the establishment was trying to do, while keeping Bustamante in prison, was to play Manley off against Bustamante and build him up in the eyes of the workers as their new leader. The *Gleaner* in particular was full of praise for the work that Manley was doing on behalf of the workers. In an article captioned 'Towards a Glorious Dawn', a *Gleaner* columnist portrayed Manley as the workers' saviour:

> Regardless of what monetary increase, what better working conditions, what holiday and sick leave any of them may now receive,

the gaining of Mr. Manley as leader remains their biggest win . . . Labour has found its place in the sun. And now that Labour has found a good, a proper leader the way is clear for the amelioration of working conditions . . . Mr. Manley is, and always has been every working man's friend . . . There is ahead a glorious dawn. The dawn of a new day for every labourer.[76]

Later in the afternoon of May 26 Manley had another meeting with the Governor at which the latter again refused to consider the release of Bustamante, but offered what he regarded as an important concession. He announced the appointment of a Board of Conciliation with terms of reference:

(a)   to receive and enquire into representations by employers and employees in regard to existing labour disputes with the object of bringing about immediate settlement so as to secure continuation of work;

(b) to make recommendations in the light of information obtained . . . with a view to the establishment of permanent machinery whereby such disputes can be investigated and settled;

(c)   to make recommendations which will assist to relieve unemployment and for social legislation affecting the labour classes generally.[77]

Twenty-Three

Manley's Labour Committee

It is difficult to say, in retrospect, exactly how Norman Manley's mind was working at this time. On the one hand, as he stated in his diary (written up on June 11), he had advised the Governor to release Bustamante from as early as the very night on which the latter had been arrested. On the other hand, when the Governor refused to do so, Manley seems to have reconciled himself to this position. He had accordingly advised the waterfront workers, on May 26, to accept the employers' offer and return to work while Bustamante and Grant were still in prison.

When he saw the Governor on May 26 and reported that the workers were holding out for Bustamante's release and the Governor again refused to release him, Manley did not make any public reference to this. In his statement to the press later that afternoon he said that he was 'very glad that Government, in keeping with its promise on representations made by those of us who are working in labour's interests — and I believe supported by the employer interests — has appointed a Conciliation Commission'. He then proceeded to explain his plans for establishing a Labour Committee and to invite volunteers to help with its work. This is how he worded his appeal:

> Now is the opportunity for Labour to organise itself, and to secure fullest consideration of its problems, and to strengthen its position forever. There may never be such an opportunity again for many years to come . . .
> . . . the object of the Labour Committee that I am trying to form is first of all to represent the different groups of workers before the Conciliation Board and to negotiate on their behalf. Secondly to deal with the organisation of Trade Unions, and thirdly to prepare and advocate a programme for the general improvement of labour conditions.

One of the most important tasks of the Committee is to draw up a programme for labour reform and to try and lay a foundation for a genuine Labour Party in Jamaica. It is hoped that the labour programme will be ready for publication within a day.

Manley then indicated the sort of assistance he wanted:

I am appealing . . . to any persons who are sincerely on the side of labour and willing to join me in forming a Labour Committee to communicate with me or come to see me at 10 o'clock tomorrow morning [Friday] . . . there will be great need for workers because the work of representing the cause of labour before the commission will require the appointment of committees to deal with different branches of the matters that have to be considered. I am also asking that all labour groups who have been in touch with me should appoint two or three representatives and should get in touch with me tomorrow morning so that we can consider the next steps to be taken. I wish particularly to see the representatives of the ship and dock labourers so that the next move can be considered for tomorrow.[78]

How should one interpret the formation of this Labour Committee by Manley? As is evident from his memoirs, the 'ugly frame of mind' of the workers which he had sensed on his 'perambulations' around the city on May 24 had disturbed him. He had also deplored the 'confusion and disorder endangering innocent people's lives, destroying property and compelling Government to call out armed forces'. The institutionalisation of the working class struggle would obviously be preferable, from his point of view, to the spontaneous, unorganised, indisciplined and sometimes violent upheaval which was still running its course in Jamaica at the end of May.

Two of the functions of the Labour Committee were directly concerned with the wages and working conditions of the workers. Firstly, there was the function of the negotiation of immediate wage increases, reduction of working hours and improvement of working conditions. This function had to be performed immediately as thousands of workers were still out on strike. Secondly there was the function of forming trade unions, which would take over the task of negotiating with the employers after they had become established. The immediate negotiating function was clearly an 'ad hoc' task, but how was the Labour Committee going to relate to the new trade unions which it expected to organise or assist to come into being? And was it to continue to exist after it had performed its initial tasks? Finally, what role did Manley see for himself personally in the new trade union movement?

Manley had accepted the invitation to attend the meeting of waterfront workers which had been fixed for the morning of May 27, with a view to the formation of a waterfront workers union with Bustamante as its President. It is therefore reasonable to assume that he did not go to that meeting with any intention of competing for the presidency. Nor is it likely that he would have desired to hold office in any of the other trade unions which were expected to come into existence. That he should wish to be free to appear for various groups of workers in wage negotiations during the current emergency would be understandable to most employers, but it would be an entirely different matter if he were to become an officer of the trade union movement. Apart from any other considerations, there were many companies for which he held general retainers. It therefore seems probable that Manley saw his role to be merely that of an adviser, albeit a most influential adviser, and an advocate serving the workers, and the functions of his Labour Committee as temporary.

Our Marxist group decided to cooperate with the Labour Committee and accordingly I attended the first meeting at Manley's chambers on Friday May 27. It was an extraordinary gathering. Whilst most of those present no doubt genuinely desired to see that the workers' standard of living was improved, some may have been more concerned to devise ways and means of dampening down the working class upsurge and rendering the proposed trade unions ineffective. One such person I recall was a European named Baltaxe.

Working on the naive assumption that there would have to be a vote by the members of a union before a strike could take place, this man advocated an idea which he thought would make strikes impossible. He proposed that all workers should be organised in one union so that if the workers in a particular work place or industry had a wage dispute in progress and wanted to strike, their strike proposal would be out voted by workers in other work places or industries who might have no claims or disputes current at that particular time. No one paid this proposal much attention.

No. 2 Pier. Busta's release, May 28th 1938.

Twenty-Four

Bustamante's Release

The meeting of waterfront workers at No. 1 Railway Pier on the morning of Friday May 27 was again largely attended and on this occasion the press were not excluded. The workers listened to the proposal for the formation of a union and to solicitor Livingston's assurance that Bustamante had approved it and was willing to be their President. The proposal was greeted with tremendous enthusiasm, but they were angry that bail had again been refused. Manley, who was listened to respectfully, had obviously been upset by the leaflet circulated at Thursday morning's meeting, which it appears he had only just seen. He described it as 'scurrilous' and was reported to have answered the accusation that he was acting as a 'tool of the capitalists' in the following terms:

> It is perfectly true that as a lawyer I represent a great number of companies, but I do not represent more companies than I represent poor people in our law courts. And it is because of this advantage that I am able to go and speak on your behalf to men who will trust me to put your cause fairly.

He also said: 'I have never advised you against your interests. It is an offer that has been made, nobody need accept it . . . I have done my best . . .'

Manley then went on to disavow any interest in politics. The *Gleaner* quoted him as saying: 'I am not going in for politics. I have no time to go in for politics. I hope there will be no jealousy and suspicion on this cause'. This disavowal of an interest in politics at this time is curious, as he had by then already been persuaded of the need for a political party. Perhaps he meant that he had nothing personal to gain? The statement, if correctly reported, is difficult to understand. Many workers present expressed disapproval of the leaflet, but when, according to the *Gleaner,* 'Mr. Manley asked whether they were prepared to sign a document pledging their support to the Union they were unanimous in their resolve to do nothing until their leader Mr. Alexander Bustamante and St. William Grant were out of prison'.[79]

On this point all that Manley could say was: 'I only hope that there will be good news from the Court today'. He was referring to the fact that yet another attempt to get bail was to be made, though in fact it was not until the following day that the prisoners were brought before the High Court on a Writ of Habeas Corpus. But Manley may have known more than he was willing or able to disclose. The probabilities are that the course of events had made the Governor realise that there was no way he was going to break the strike, that so long as Bustamante remained in prison labour unrest was likely to increase and that there was no possibility of driving a wedge between Manley and Bustamante.

Arrangements were made for the application to be heard before Bertram (Bumpy) Burrowes, a Jamaican who was then an acting High Court Judge. He was a practical man with some understanding and sympathy for the new spirit that was now alive in Jamaica. It is possible that the word had been quietly passed down from King's House that Bustamante and Grant were to be released. And Judge Burrowes did indeed grant the application for bail when the matter came before him at a specially arranged session of the Court on Saturday May 28. The Courts were not normally open for business on a Saturday. Nevertheless, the proprieties were duly observed. Manley filed an affidavit stating that he was satisfied that everything was now calm and that if Bustamante were to be released 'no disorder will arise'. Other affidavits said much the same. The Acting Attorney General then solemnly informed the Court that, on the basis of the assurances given, the Crown was now willing to withdraw its opposition to bail. It was all a ridiculous charade. There had, in fact, been no decrease in popular unrest, and would have been none whilst Bustamante's imprisonment continued. It was indeed because of the militancy and determination of the workers that the release of Bustamante and Grant was achieved.

The two men were bailed to attend before the Resident Magistrate in Kingston on June 1. So far as I am aware, they did not do so, unless it was at an unpublicised session. Subsequently, on June 6, the Acting Governor consulted his Privy Council where it was suggested that if

Bustamante and Grant would undertake not to cause a breach of peace, all charges should be dropped. On June 15 the Privy Council advised that a 'nolle prosequi' be entered and this was accordingly done.[80]

Deputation for Busta's release to Headquarters House, May 1939.

Twenty-Five

The Situation In
St. James

The situation at Montego Bay had meanwhile become very tense on May 27. Two contradictory developments had contributed to this. On the one hand the Custos, owner of Barnet Sugar Estate, and the Inspector of Police had spent the day enrolling a hundred middle and upper class young men as Special Constables and police reinforcements had been brought to the town. On the other hand, representatives of the principal employers were meeting with representatives of the Jamaica Workers and Tradesmen's Union (J.W.T.U.) to discuss the workers' demands for wage increases.

The J.W.T.U. team was led by A.G.S. Coombs assisted by L.O. Alberga and C.B. Chambers. Chambers was a clerk employed on one of the wharves and was an officer of both the J.W.T.U. and the Northern Clerks Association. Alberga, as far as I can recall, was self-employed but had volunteered to assist the workers because of his political convictions. While in the U.S.A. in 1932 he had been recruited to go to the Soviet Union to act in a film. And although that was a time of hardship in the world's first socialist state, he had seen enough, even at that early stage, to realise that the future of mankind would be moulded by the working class. When the meeting at Montego Bay ended it was announced that agreement had been reached on the rates to be paid for loading bananas and that the fruit for export would be brought to the port on the following Monday. The *Gleaner* on May 28 stated: 'It is likely that the strike here will terminate very shortly.[81]

Under the headline 'Montego Bay Labourers Get All — round Pay Increase', the next issue of the *Daily Gleaner* reported that the strike had been settled. Boatmen loading bananas were to receive an increase of 2/6d (25¢) per 1000 stems, bringing them up to 30/- ($3.00) per 1000. New rates were agreed for wharf workers — for loading dye-wood and sugar 1/3d (12½¢) per ton, for rum 9d (7½¢) per puncheon and for lumber 2/- (20¢) and 1/6d (15¢) according to the load. Banana carriers were to receive 2/ 3d (22½¢) instead of 2/- (20¢) per 100 stems, the increase being retrospective to May 23; day labour men 3/6d (35¢) instead of 3/- (30¢) with overtime rates at 10d (8 1/3¢) instead of 8d per hour; rail car unloaders 4/6d (45¢) instead of 3/9d (37½¢). Stevedores handling bananas were to get 36/10d (just under $3.69) instead of 31/10d per 1000 stems. The waterworks labourers had been reluctant to accept the 2/6d (25¢) per day negotiated, but had decided to accept it for the time being upon the union agreeing to send a telegram demanding more.

Meanwhile, cane field and factory workers were reported, on May 28, to be still on strike in Vere, Clarendon, as were wharf workers at Bowden and at Manchioneal in Portland. Railway linesmen in the Albany section in St. Mary had come out on strike demanding 5/- (50¢) per day.[82]

Twenty-Six

The Conciliation Board

After his release at about mid-day on Saturday May 28, Bustamante had what he described as a 'brief' meeting with the Conciliation Board. He arrived at No. 1 Railway Pier shortly after 4 p.m. with Norman Manley, J.A.G. Smith, Ross Livingston and the Mayor, where a huge crowd was awaiting him. Addressing the striking waterfront workers he advised a return to work. As regards the terms on which the strike had been settled, he told the workers: 'Whilst I was in difficulties, through Mr. Manley, we succeeded in getting an increase of two pence. But I have now succeeded in getting a little more than that. The companies had decided not to give double pay for overtime except on the old rates. I have got them to agree to give double pay for overtime at the new rate. So if you get 10d per hour, your overtime will be 1/8d. If you get 11d ordinarily your overtime will be 1/10d'.

Though Bustamante claimed the credit for obtaining this increase in the overtime rates, he was not telling the truth as this had been conceded on the day previous to his release. In the same issue of the *Gleaner* in which Bustamante's remarks were reported, there was an interview with Manley in which, without taking issue with Bustamante, he clarified the matter:

> On Wednesday the wharf owners and shipping agents had agreed to raise the rates of pay by two pence an hour day work, overtime rates remaining unchanged. This offer was rejected by the men who at the same time insisted that they would stand on strike until such time as Mr. Bustamante was released. Late on Thursday the Conciliation Board was appointed and all Friday the Board was working with interviews with myself and with the dock owners and shipping agents. It was through mediation of the Board that the dock owners and shipping agents raised their offer so as to include double overtime on the two pence increase.

Bustamante's obvious purpose was to impress his audience with the belief that, in a matter of minutes after his release, he had been able to get just that little extra for them that Manley had been unable to achieve in prolonged negotiations. There would be many other instances of Bustamante's cunning in the years ahead.

That same day the Conciliation Board announced that, at its instance, the fruit companies had agreed to increased rates for workers carrying and loading bananas on the wharves and aboard ship. Dock labourers including those discharging bananas from railway cars would have their pay per thousand stems increased from 5/10d to 6/8d (66 2/3¢) for fruit for Europe and from 6/8d to 7/6d (75¢) for the more mature fruit going to Canada. Banana carriers' pay would go up from 2/- (20¢) to 2/3d (22½¢) per 100 stems. Stackers of fruit who had earned 8d would get 10d per hour and stevedores' pay would go up from the present rate of 30/- ($3.00) per 1000 stems to 35/- ($3.50) for fruit for Europe and from 35/- to 40/- ($4.00) for fruit for Canada.[83]

For the next month the Conciliation Board was to be the principal forum for the consideration and settlement of claims for wage increases and improved hours and conditions of employment. The *Gleaner* reported that on Monday May 30 Bustamante and Manley 'were here there and everywhere about the city'. In a statement to the newspapers Manley reported:

> Today was a busy day . . . The effort to put an end to existing strikes with the assistance of the Conciliation Board has met with further signal success. I, together with Mr. Bustamante, represented, on behalf of the daily labourers of the Public Works Department who have not been receiving a wage higher than 3/- per day for a fifty percent increase in wages, for a reduction of the ten hour day to a nine hour day, for a minimum half day's wage where work is prevented by rain, for weekly payment instead of . . . fortnightly . . . and for assistance in transportation in the Corporate area where work is being done at far distances from the town itself.

Agreement was reached on an increase in the basic daily rate to 3/9d (37½¢); a nine hour working day with one hour off for lunch; and a guaranteed half day's pay when work which had been arranged was stopped or prevented by rain. The transport question was deferred for further consideration. These terms, said Manley, were put to a mass meeting in Trench Town and accepted unanimously by the workers.

Twenty-Seven

The Countryside Erupts

But if Manley was correct in suggesting that labour unrest was subsiding in the Kingston area, the picture in the rural areas was very different. The *Gleaner* headlined the fact that 'From All Over the Island Reports Come In of Labour Strikes'.[84] In the rural parishes the workers, with new found confidence, stepped up their demands for wage increases and refused to be intimidated. Everywhere workers were fighting back even when confronted by armed force. The official Report catalogues a series of strikes and disorders between May 28 and June 10, some of which are mentioned below.[85]

There were disorders at Grantham and Frankfield in Clarendon on the evening of May 28. The main road from Hectors River to Manchioneal in Portland was blocked by boulders and trees on the night of May 29 and in some places telegraph lines were cut. Armed local forces from Spanish Town were sent to Santa Cruz in St. Elizabeth and two platoons of British soldiers were sent to Mandevile in view of anticipated strikes. Armed forces were also sent on that day to Savanna-la-Mar and Frome in Westmoreland, also in anticipation of strikes.

On May 30, though strikers at West Indies Sugar Company properties in Clarendon returned to work, other workers in Vere in the same parish came out on strike. The police drove off strikers at Sevens Estate near May Pen who endeavoured to prevent other workers from returning to work. 'On Whitney property a crowd of four hundred tenants and labourers . . . stopped all work: they carried away bananas and damaged a bridge'.

In Manchester during the nights of May 29 and 30 barricades blocked the main road between Williamsfield and Mandeville. On May 30 'Mobs began to collect in Mandeville from 9 a.m. onwards from the surrounding districts armed with sticks and cutlasses. Some shops closed and others were forced to do so . . . The crowds were dispersed by the police and military but so soon as that had been done they re-formed somewhere else . . . Hotels and private houses were entered and food and money demanded; roads on the outskirts of the town were blocked. Early in the afternoon a detachment of Sherwood Foresters [the British regiment stationed in Jamaica at the time] drove the main crowd down the Mandeville Hill with fixed bayonets'.

Strikers were out in force on that day also at various points in St. Elizabeth and the local forces that had been sent to Frome were brought back to Santa Cruz. In St. James labourers employed by the Public Works Department refused to work. Also on May 30 'on practically all the large banana growing estates [in St. Mary] strikes occurred but there was very little disorder. In Annotto Bay strikers went from property to property intimidating any labourers found at work'.

In Portland strikers assembled in large numbers in the square at Port Antonio and at Manchioneal, where the employees of the Standard Fruit Company 'demanded an increase of pay and assaulted the local representative of the Company'. Another official of this company was set upon near Hectors River and his car was damaged. Shops were looted at Flat Grass and Belle Castle. Numerous trucks carrying bananas to be loaded for export at Port Antonio were turned back. A platoon of British soldiers were sent to clear road blocks between Manchioneal and Morant Bay in St. Thomas.[86]

Here and there the establishment was still able to assert its authority. The *Daily Gleaner* of May 31 reported that at Savanna-la-Mar the trial of the second batch of thirty-one Frome strikers had ended with conviction of thirteen of their number and the imposition of prison sentences of six months, two months and thirty days. Meanwhile the trial of a third batch of twenty-one of these workers charged with rioting was under way. Special Constables were on an intimidatory rampage in certain areas. But for the most part the initiative remained with the workers.

Reporting on the situation on May 31 in the rural areas, the headlines and sub-headlines in the *Daily Gleaner* read:

Labour Unrest Still Holds Jamaica in its Grip
Road and Agricultural Workers are Not Yet Appeased
Shut Down Business at Montego Bay[87]

Police were sent on May 31 to disperse a crowd and clear a barricade blocking the road to Whitney in Manchester. Roads were blocked again in St. Elizabeth. In St. James 'strikes were general throughout the parish and in Montego Bay crowds collected and forced the shops to close'. Two platoons of local forces were sent to the town. Crowds were marching again in St. Mary at Port Maria and Annotto Bay. In Buff Bay Portland, 'a large crowd . . . forced all shops to close'. In St. Thomas 'strikes took place on almost all properties not already affected'. A demonstration near Bath was broken up by the Police.[88]

On June 1 a military patrol from Mandeville had to be rushed to Whitney where there was again trouble and that night yet another barricade was erected cutting off the estate. Also in Clarendon, at Rock River, the road was blocked and a tank belonging to a fruit export firm was damaged. More roads were blocked in Manchester. Strikers at Raheen in St. Elizabeth, who had occupied the factory yard, were driven out by a mixed force of military and police. Strikers manning road blocks at Balaclava were fired on by the military but only one person reported receiving gun-shot wounds. On this day the workers at Prospect factory in Hanover joined the strike, as did cane cutters at Tilston in Trelawny. Strikers marching from Esher to Highgate in St. Mary were blocked and scattered by an armed force.

There were clashes between demonstrators and the police and the military on June 2 at St. Jago property in Clarendon; on the main road from Lacovia to Magotty and at Balaclava in St. Elizabeth; at Prospect in Hanover; and at Hampden in Trelawny. 'In the morning a crowd of four hundred or so marched from Harmony in St. Mary through Highgate to Richmond and from there to Charlottenburgh . . . They stopped all work in the district and took away the tools of any labourers found at work. In Richmond the police took back the tools . . . but were not sufficiently numerous to disperse the crowd who turned to looting shops, throwing stones and blocking the streets with rubbish. The crowd then went back to Highgate blocking the road behind them and continued looting there until the police who had been reinforced by a patrol of the Sherwood Foresters were able to disperse them. At the same time another mob was behaving in a similar manner at Maiden Hall in the Gayle area [in the same parish] and the police . . . were unable to cope with it. The Inspector in charge of the party was attacked and received injuries . . . and his car was badly damaged . . .'

In St. Thomas 'Strikes continued on a number of properties. At Duckenfield sugar estate labourers struck and, arming themselves with cutlasses and sticks, became very threatening. However upon the arrival of an armed party of police they dispersed'.[89] That same day Governor Denham was taken ill suddenly and died after an emergency operation.

Twenty-Eight

Focus On St. Mary —
Police Brutality

Meanwhile, in an effort to calm the situation in the rural areas, the Con ciliation Board switched its attention to the claims of agricultura workers in St. Mary. The following new minimum rates of wages were recommended by the Board on June 1:

Banana cutters	—	1/3d (12½¢) per 100 stems
Heading bananas	—	various rates of ½d, 1d, 1½d and 2d per stem according to distance, etc.
Forking	—	2/9d (27½¢) per square chain (22 yards
Cleaning trenches	—	6d (5¢) per chain
Digging new trenches (2ft. x 2ft. x 1ft)	—	1/9d (17½¢) per chain
'Dropping' suckers (a planting operation)	—	1/- (10¢) per 100 suckers
Day labour	—	3/- (30¢) per day plus 4d (3 1/3¢) per hour overtime
Women labourers	—	1/3d (12½¢) per day
Salaried headmen	—	10 percent increases on existing rates[90]

Manley and Bustamante then signed a joint appeal to banana workers in St. Mary which was published on the following day. The appeal stated:

> They were present at the meeting of the Conciliation Board on June 1 and the scale of rates was debated for a whole day. The rate published in the newspapers on June 2 were agreed upon by them as the best they could succeed in obtaining for the workers. The beg to ask that all workers accept these rates and return to work and that they should realise that a good deal has been obtained and

more cannot be obtained at present.

N.W. Manley   A. Bustamante[91]

The unrest in St. Mary was not, however, assuaged by the Conciliation Board's proceedings because of the particularly brutal activity of the Police at Islington on that same day. A party of police fired on a crowd of strikers, killing four and wounding others. The names of the dead were Caleb Barrett, Archibald Franklin, Felix McLaglen and Thadeus Smith. Among the wounded was Nathaniel Senior.[92] But of all the acts of police brutality on that day at Islington, their attack on a brave and powerful striker by the name of Edgar Daley was the worst. These cavalier executions and the brutal treatment of Daley which crippled him for life, so enraged the whole community that soon afterwards a detachment of British soldiers from the Sherood Foresters regiment was moved into the area to suppress the angry reactions. They found that the telephone wires had been cut. According to the official report, they 'encountered some resistance from unruly crowds'.

Daley had been armed with a stick which he refused to surrender when threatened by an armed policeman. 'No, not a rass!' he is alleged to have said defiantly, 'You have your gun I have my stick'. When he threw a policeman to the ground, he was bayonetted and his back was broken by blows from rifle buts.[93] He was never able to work again and died, a pauper, in the Alms House. Years later a monument was erected at Islington to those who were killed on that day.

Twenty-Nine

Unrest In Other Areas

On the same day that these events were taking place in St. Mary telephone wires were cut between Newport and Mandeville in Manchester and near Davis's Cove in Hanover and the road was blocked for about a mile with boulders and trees in the latter area. A police party which went to the district to make arrests was stoned and some of the party were injured. The main road from Kingston was blocked by a barricade at Lime Hall in St. Ann.

During this whole period, though there were shootings by the military and police which resulted in some deaths and large numbers being wounded and despite hundreds of arrests, strikes and demonstrations in the rural areas had been steadily increasing. June 6, according to the official Report 'was the worst day in the parishes when the disorders reached their climax'. That day the Acting Governor, fearing that the rising tide of resistance to the armed forces could not be contained, sent a cable requesting that another company of the Sherwood Foresters regiment, stationed in Bermuda, be sent to Jamaica.

The official Report stated further that 'Throughout the day, the Sherwood Foresters, taking advantage of the presence of the detachment of Royal Marines at Up-Park Camp . . . undertook an extended system of patrols covering the parishes of Clarendon, Manchester, St. Ann, St. Mary and Portland'. The resistance of strikers at Worthy Park to attempts by the soldiers to disperse them was particularly stubborn and on two occasions the soldiers fired on the workers, wounding several persons.

In Westmoreland also 'Further strikes occurred and some demonstrations were made in various parts of the parish'. So widespread was the unrest in Westmoreland that two platoons of British soldiers were sent to Savanna-la-Mar, arriving soon after day-break on June 7. At Lucea, in Hanover 'a large crowd gathered about 9.30 a.m. and marched

Hanover St. May 23rd 1938.

through the town carrying sticks and flags'. Strikers manning a road block at Jericho were fired on and at least one was wounded.

At Tryall in St. James strikers who had occupied the estate yard were fired on and a woman was killed and at least one person was wounded. Police used batons to break up a crowd of demonstrators at Ducketts estate who had stopped all work there. At Ulster Spring in Trelawny an armed party went to Stetin to rescue the estate owner and supervisory staff who had been blockaded in the great house, but found themselves ambushed on their return by a crowd above the road who rolled boulders down the hill upon them. When they reached the main road they were confronted by another crowd upon whom they fired killing one and wounding others. During some of these encounters in the western parts of the island a sea-plane from HMS 'Ajax', which had been sent to Montego Bay, was used to 'buzz' and intimidate the strikers and demonstrators.

Near Claremont in St. Ann on June 6 demonstrators succeeded in rescuing some of the workers who had been arrested by the police. When a military patrol arrived more arrests were made. On June 7 trigger-happy patrols of Special Constables fired on a small crowd at Hopewell and another at Cascade in Hanover. Three men were officially reported to have been wounded. Another such patrol wounded a boy at Johns Hall in St. James. Other incidents occurred over the next three days and there were more shootings, but according to the official report 'there was no serious disorder after the 10th of June'. A further company of British troops nevertheless arrived on June 20.[94]

Thirty

The Peasants Demand Land

During this period it was not only the wage earners who had got up off their knees and demanded improvements rather than begging for them. Peasants too, as we have seen, were standing proud, discarding the traditional method of supplication by petition and making demands on large land owners and the government for land and for the abolition of rents.

On May 25 the *Jamaica Standard* had reported that, as a result of the activities of the peasant organisation led by Robert E. Rumble, tenants of large land owners in upper Clarendon had been refusing to pay rents. The newspaper reported that the association, the P.M.I.L.-S.L.A., told these small tenant farmers that 'rightful ownership' of the land had been given to their forebears at emancipation and that ninety-nine years leases, by virtue of which the landlords held the land, would expire on August 1, the anniversary of emancipation. The newspaper alleged that some small farmers, in anticipation of their acquisition of formal ownership, were offering to pay taxes in advance and were putting up fences.[95]

The same story is told in a minute of an interview at the Colonial Office in June 1938 with John Miller, a pen-keeper with lands in Manchester and Clarendon. On the basis of that interview a Colonial Office official wrote:

> There was a story going around among the labourers ... that Queen Victoria in 1838 had granted the land to estate owners for one hundred years; after that it was to be divided up amongst the people. Labourers who rented plots from the estates were being organised in order to secure their 'rights' on 1st August. In the Clarendon district there had been a no-rent campaign since the beginning of the year, and labourers have already staked out their plots and endeavoured to induce Government tax-collectors to accept land-tax on these plots in order to establish a claim to them at zero hour. It is said that owners who will not hand over are to be massacred. (I

understand that a similar story was told to Sir H. Moore by the Bishop of Jamaica yesterday). If this is true it would explain the anxiety of the Officer administering the Government to have a warship available on 1st August.[96]

The exact form in which Rumble relayed to these small tenant farmers his message that, one hundred years after the abolition of slavery, the payment of rent to the big land owners should cease, is by no means clear. The fact that when slavery was abolished in 1838 the slave owners had received compensation but the slaves had got nothing had been a long-standing cause of resentment in Jamaica. What was clear to the Government, and sent shivers down the spine of every large land owner, was that this message, whatever its form, could easily spread throughout the island. Rumble therefore had to be silenced. He was accordingly arrested and charged with committing an act of public mischief, an indictable offence. Rumble's 'acts' were all words. There were seven counts to the indictment which charged that Rumble:

> at divers dates between the 31st July and 2nd September 1938 at Cupids, Rose Hill, Crooked River and divers other places . . . in the parish of Clarendon . . . did incite his hearers . . . some . . . on some occasions and others on other occasions, to enter upon and take possession of land without any legal right to do so and did incite tenants to abstain from the payment of rent lawfully due and to resist the lawful excution of distress for arrears of such rent .
> [97]

Rumble's subsequent trial at Chapleton in Clarendon lasted for three days, ending on December 27, 1938. He was sentenced to six months hard labour on each of the seven counts, the sentences to run concurrently. The report described him as 'a diminutive thirty-two year old tenant cultivator', but there was nothing diminutive about his ideas. The Magistrate, in sentencing him, referred to his intelligence and made it quite clear that the severity of the sentence was related to this fact.

Rumble was familiar with the ideas of the American economist Henry George and his organisation had relations with the Henry George Foundation in England. After his imprisonment, a member of this body came to investigate the case and, while in Jamaica, was invited by Manley to explain George's theory to members of the P.N.P. The meeting, which I attended, took place at Manley's house "Drumblair". This is how the P.N.P. came to adopt and later introduce in

Jamaica, George's system of taxing land according to its quality in its undeveloped state rather than, as in most countries, on its value with improvements. Rumble had been the first person in Jamaica to appreciate the advantages of this system.

The cry for land was also raised in St. Ann. The official Report stated that on June 3: 'A mob of about forty armed with sticks and cutlasses invaded Greenwich Park property near St. Ann's Bay demanding land and threatening to burn the house and kill the cattle'. A party of 'armed police' was sent to the area and the invaders were 'driven out'.

Alarmed at the demand for land from landless agricultural workers and small farmers with insufficient land, the Acting Governor hurriedly announced on June 5 that a sum of half a million pounds had been set aside which was to be spent immediately for land settlement. Shortly afterwards this provision was increased by a further one hundred and fifty thousand pounds.[98] This, announced a headline in the *Gleaner,* will 'MAKE PEOPLE INDEPENDENT LANDOWNERS'[99]

Thirty-One

Royal Commission Appointed

The news of the social explosion in Jamaica had produced, almost immediately, a standard response in the Colonial Office. A memorandum by the Secretary of State for the Colonies, undated but apparently prepared after a Cabinet meeting on May 25, recorded this cynical comment: 'An early announcement that a Royal Commission was to visit the Islands would have a good psychological effect in these Colonies. It would tend to reassure their people that we here *are* keenly interested in their affairs, and anxious to do what we can to help, and it would therefore tend to calm excited feelings there'.[100] On June 10 the newspapers reported that a Royal Commission would investigate Jamaican conditions.

There had been social explosions similar to the Jamaican experience in all the British sugar colonies in the Caribbean area and the West Indies Royal Commission was required to visit them all. This time honoured device, which allowed those with grievances to air them publicly and created the impression that the British Government really intended to do something to improve the living standards of the people in the colonies, was, from the British Government's point of view, a great success. It undoubtedly bought time for imperialist interests and strengthened the illusions which their perpetuation required. The Commission, which included a well intentioned British trade union leader, arrived in Jamaica in November 1938, where, as in the other colonies, it received a considerable volume of evidence.

Thirty-Two

Formation Of Trade Unions

Let us now return to the narrative of working class organisation. After
the settlement of the Kingston waterfront workers' strike on May 28,
the next priority, according to Bustamante, was the formation of the
proposed union. 'Fellow workers', he said, 'the first thing I want you to
do next week is to send me at my office a deputation of three or four
including my friend Mr. Williams. I want to consult with Mr. Williams
and two or three others from among you. I want to shoot right ahead
with the union'.[101] In a statement issued to the press that same day he
said:

> Well known legal minds have promised to see that the constitution
> is properly drawn up, and I am hoping a draft of it will be ready for
> consideration this week.

In the same statement he said: 'Federation of labour has been one of
the dearest things to my heart and now that we have made a start, I will
see that there is no turning back'.

On June 1, 1938 I wrote to O'Meally and Domingo bringing them up
to date:

> We are pushing ahead with the formation of unions. When I cabled
> you, some of us intended to get on with it on our own as soon as we
> got enough information. Now Mr. Manley has set up a Committee
> and we are co-operating with him. The Dockmen's Union has been
> formed, with Mr. Bustamante as president. A sub-committee con-
> sisting of Messrs. E.E.A. Campbell, E.N. [sic] Nethersole, W.E.
> Foster-Davis, and myself . . . has been appointed to draft a constitu-
> tion and submit it to them.

At first Bustamante announced that he was going to organise five
trade unions and his solicitor was still speaking of this number of
unions in August. The first of these was to be the union of waterfront
workers, to be called the Maritime Union, and it was for this union that

99

the sub-committee of Manley's Labour Committee had prepared a constitution. Later the number of proposed unions was increased to seven, but when the first stationery was printed the names of only the following six were listed:

Maritime Workers Union; Transport Workers Union; Factory Workers Union; General Workers Union; Artisan Union; Municipal Workers Union.

Across the top of this stationery appeared the words BUSTAMANTE INDUSTRIAL UNIONS.[102]

This extraordinary practice of including Bustamante's name in the name of the trade union was introduced soon after his release from imprisonment. A telephone was installed in the premises he rented at 61½ Duke Street in Kingston at the beginning of June, listed in the name 'Bustamante Maritime Union'. On July 9 an advertisement, drawn up by solicitor Livingston, which contained the statement 'Look Out For The Name "Bustamante" on All His Unions', appeared in the *Jamaica Labour Weekly*.[103]

No. 2 Pier Strikers return to work after Busta's release, May 1938.

Thirty-Three

Proprietory Unionism

It is necessary to say a few words about the fate of the constitution we prepared because it illustrates very clearly Bustamante's proprietory approach to trade unionism, an approach which made a permanent imprint on the form of Jamaican trade unionism. The draft we gave to Bustamante was mainly my work. It provided for the election of officers and an executive committee. It had been assumed, quite naturally, that Bustamante would be formally elected President, but that was not what he had in mind at all. He instructed his solicitor to amend the draft so as to make him president for life, name the union after him and give him the power to appoint its managing committee. As for the funds of the union, these were to be controlled by the President 'as a sub-committee of one'!

It very soon became apparent that Bustamante did not regard a trade union as belonging to its members. Nor did he see himself in the role of a servant or employee of the workers. He conceived of a union as something more in the nature of a business and saw himself as its proprietor. The union would offer a service to the workers in return for their money and support. In Bustamante's book unionism was a straight commercial transaction.

Though initially Bustamante had intended to form a number of unions with separate names which would be known collectively as the 'Bustamante Industrial Unions', none of the seven unions whose names were announced ever enjoyed in practice a separate existence. From the start there was in fact a single organisation. This was clearly illustrated later in the oral evidence given before the West Indies Royal Commission by Bustamante and J.A.G Edwards, the acting General Secretary, when they were questioned on November 16 by Sir Walter Citrine, Secretary of the British T.U.C., about the structure of the organisation.

Or supposing they thought you were honest, would it not be a just supposition that you were merely a reactionary, sublimating the major issue of the class struggle to the immediate issue of preserving order at all costs. And if they came to that conclusion, would they not, in their minds, be doing a service by purging the movement. A reactionary at the top, however honest his purpose, is a great setback to any labour programme. If only you had made it known that the men would get everything, that very important cause of distrust would have been removed.

But more unfortunate than anything else was the theory which was common property among the people, that you were attempting to undermine Bustamante while he was in gaol. Not that Bustamante himself was so vital. But the fact was that the men had experienced two things entirely new to them — (a) coming together, (b) sticking together. And they had come together and stuck together in loyalty to one man — Bustamante. Before he was arrested Mr. Campbell had started talking about 'irresponsible agitators' etc, they feared that this was a more subtle attempt. Anyone who undermined Bustamante at that time was undermining unity, on the first occasion that it had made its appearance in Jamaica. And, to the cause, that would have been a terrific devastating blow.

Now that this serious misunderstanding has been removed, and if this movement is to be real, not entirely monopolised by middle and upper class control as there is a danger that every new movement may easily be; and if you will only accept it, you have the assistance of active, influential *and above all sincere* men in these your most recent opponents. All that is necessary is that you should direct it on the right lines, and that you insure that it is not clogged with reactionaries from the start. Many will rush forward to help, who, if allowed, will set up something eminently respectable, but, on analysis, anti-labour. I do not suggest that such men's assistance should be rudely refused, but control must be kept out of their hands.

I earnestly hope that you will accept my explanation of the conduct of these men, in the same spirit that they have accepted my explanation of yours. Unity, particularly at the beginning, is strength. I must apologise for the length of this, but it is short in proportion to its importance.

Yours sincerely
Richard Hart

Thirty-Six

What Kind of
Political Party

In the period up to the middle of 1938 the primary concern of the Marx-ist group had been the formation of trade unions. We conceived of these as weapons of the working class in their direct economic struggle against the capitalists, foreign and local, who controlled the economy. We also subscribed to the view expressed by Marx and Engels that the trade unions can serve as 'schools of solidarity' and 'schools of socialism', and to the resolution proposed by Marx and approved at the Congress of the International Workingmen's Association as far back as 1868 which had stated:

> In addition to their original tasks, the trade unions must now learn how to act consciously as focal points for organising the working class in the greater interests of its complete emancipation. They must support every social and political movement directed towards this aim.[109]

This was later to become an issue when, in pursuance of the recom-mendations of the 1938 Royal Commission, the British Government started sending out 'Labour Advisers' to the colonies. These gen-tlemen, despite the fact that many of them were recruited from trade unions affiliated to the British Labour Party, made every effort to per-suade trade unionists in the colonies to have nothing to do with politics!

But, granted that it was appropriate for the working class move-ment to be involved in political activity, what should be the focus of that activity? In the debate in the columns of *Public Opinion* already men-tioned I had argued initially that self government, as proposed by the Jamaica Progressive League of New York, could prove to be an illusion and that the transition to socialism should be our immediate objective But Buchanan had helped me to get my priorities right. 'A powerfu workers' and peasants' movement is destined to rise here, having as its goal — Socialism', he wrote, but there were immediate objectives which would first have to be achieved. Our political priority must be the struggle against British imperialism.

O'Meally had also disagreed with me:

> In advanced countries the struggle is between the Capitalists and the Proletariat. In backward countries we still have an overwhelmingly large peasantry, no manufacturing activities, hardly any proletariat, and an oppressed and capitalistically underdeveloped bourgeoisie, whose political and industrial advancement has been suppressed by the Imperialists. The peasant has a great attachment to his land and livestock; the bourgeois, although he is not so strongly attached to his land as the peasant, will always defend the abstract principle of the right to private property. Since the proletariat is a negligible quantity in Jamaica, the conditions necessary for a new economic system are non existent . . .

Replying to O'Meally I had pointed out that there was a sizeable agricultural proletariat, and that he had over-estimated the conservatism of the peasant which, I had argued, 'is directly proportionate to the amount of land he owns and [in Jamaica] I seriously doubt that (with the exception of certain districts . . .) he owns much'. Another flaw in O'Meally's argument was that the revolutionary proletariat would not be expected initially to propose collectivisation in agriculture but would demand the distribution of more land to the peasants, thereby forging an alliance with them against the big landlords.

Nevertheless, the main point made by Buchanan and O'Meally, and also by Domingo and McBean when they joined the debate, was sound. An under-developed colonial country must first break the stranglehold of imperialism before the transition to socialism can be placed on the agenda.[110] With that point settled, our Marxist group still had to reach a conclusion on what would be the best form of political organisation during the anti-imperialist stage of our struggle. Our objective would be to mobilise the widest possible opposition to the imperialists and bring together, for this purpose, representatives of all the social strata oppressed or impeded by imperialism. The question was, what organisational form should this anti-imperialist front take?

One possibility was that our group could launch a workers' party guided by Marxist-Leninist theory, which would then seek to establish an alliance in pursuance of common objectives with other political groups representative of other social strata. The other was that we

111

could help to create a single broad nationalistic party within which, while preserving our separate identity, we would co-operate with nationalistic petty-bourgeois and bourgeois elements. This was a subject for urgent discussion within our group, especially after it became known that Norman Manley had agreed to Fairclough's proposal that he (Manley) should take the initiative in forming a political party.

The decision we reached was that, given the social structure of Jamaica and the prevailing circumstances, the best form for the anti-imperialist front to take would be a single political party which would seek to enrol under its banner representatives of all the social strata oppressed or impeded by British imperialism. These strata were envisaged to be the skilled and unskilled wage earners, the artisans, the small farmers, the professional middle classes and the small businessmen.

In my letter of June 1 1938 to O'Meally, I informed our New York comrades of what was about to happen on the political front and the decision we had taken:

> Mr. Manley and Mr. Fairclough are engaged in the formation of a Labour Party . . . It will be the duty of all earnest members of the movement to keep it really alive from within, and that is the line we of the left have decided to take.

May 23rd 1938, march on East Queen St.

Thirty-Seven

Evolution Of Manley's Political Views

It would be a mistake to think of Norman Manley as a person who made his entry into politics with his views on political independence and votes for all already fully developed. That his nationalistic ideas were still undergoing a process of hesitant formation and development in the latter part of 1938 is illustrated in the oral evidence which he gave before the West Indies Royal Commission. The Commission's terms of reference had been designed to exclude consideration of alterations to the existing Crown Colony constitutions or the restricted franchise on which such elections as were permitted in these colonies took place. But although this had discouraged the submission of proposals in writing for constitutional reform, some of the Commissioners found a way of getting around this obstacle when taking oral evidence from persons whose views they particularly wanted to hear.

Manley was a signatory to two memoranda submitted to the Commission — a memorandum prepared jointly with N.N. Nethersole and Dr. W.E. McCulloch and a memorandum on behalf of Jamaica Welfare Limited, a social welfare organisation of which he (Manley) was chairman, originally funded by a cess on banana exports agreed to by the United Fruit Company. Neither memorandum contained proposals for altering the constitution or the franchise, but Manley's views on these questions were solicited and expressed orally when he appeared before the Commissioners on November 14, 1938. Some of these exchanges were very revealing.

The first Commissioner who succeeded in slipping into the evidence considerations of purely political questions was Sir Walter Citrine, General Secretary of the British Trades Union Congress. His opening question with its preface was:

Q.   You are aware that the terms of reference of the Commission preclude any general consideration of what might be called the more abstract question of the political aspect of the franchise? We have to limit ourselves to the effect of the franchise upon economic and social conditions. Can the mass of the people of Jamaica, at the present time, bring any effective pressure to bear upon the members of the Legislative Council, to secure better education, better social services, better provision against unemployment?

Rising to the bait, Manley replied:

A.   Not by the ordinary constitutional means. After all, if they have not got votes, they cannot very well bring effective pressure. They can only bring the sort of pressure brought earlier this year, by public disorder.

But when Citrine and other Commissioners gave him an opportunity to clinch this point by advocating self government with full adult suffrage, Manley was hesitant. He came out against immediate self government and accepted adult suffrage without a literacy test only after he had been coaxed into it by the Commissioners. This is how the exchange developed:

Q   [Sir W. Citrine] Would you say that the state of political advancement of the people of Jamaica is such that self-government could be conferred in any full sense, at the present time?

A.   It is my opinion that it should not be conferred immediately.

Q.   [Sir W. Citrine] What test then would you feel might be applied for, say an extension of the franchise?

A.   I understand the present test for voting is the payment of a tax of 10/- per year. I am also in favour of the widest possible franchise because I think the results secured by the limited franchise are so bad, that any change must necessarily not be a change for the worse.

Q.   [Sir P. Mackinnon] Universally?

A.   I am quite prepared to see it based on a literacy test.

Q.   (Sir W Citrine] That is the point. You think a literacy test might be applied? In other words, the potential voter must show that he can read and write?

A.   Yes . . .

Q.   [The Chairman] But the point is that a literacy test is by no means easy to apply without oppression.

115

A.   Please, understand that I am giving an entirely individual opinion that is contrary to the majority of opinion at present in Jamaica. I would be quite content to see adult suffrage.

Q.   [Sir W. Citrine] Without any test at all?

A.   Without any test.

Q.   [Mr. Assheton] In your opinion, would not adult suffrage without any test, be better than adult suffrage with a literacy test?

A.   Very probably, yes.[111]

So Norman Manley, with a little prodding from members of the Commission, had finally come out in favour of full adult suffrage. His hesitancy is interesting. Reservations concerning the capacity of the masses to chose their representatives were a not uncommon middle class reaction at that time. But it is interesting to note that, only one month later, the Legislative Council voted in favour of universal suffrage. The motion was proposed by J.A.G. Smith, KC, the member for Clarendon, and approved on December 13 by twelve votes to one, the officials abstaining. According to the *Gleaner* of December 14, 1938, even the conservative nominated member Sir William Morrison supported the motion.

Thirty-Eight

Launching Of The P.N.P.

Fairclough and Norman Manley had originally proposed that the party they were planning to form should be called the 'Labour Party'. This did not mean that they had in mind a purely working class party. The choice of this name had been made originally by Fairclough and indicated no more than his approval of the pragmatic right wing social democratic leaders of the British Labour Party and his intention that the party should be seen to have an affinity with them. Norman Manley would have shared this desire. In the event, however, the name chosen was the 'Peoples National Party', a name which more accurately reflected the broader nature of the organisation. From the time of its formation the P.N.P. embraced representatives of all social strata oppressed, impeded or frustrated by imperialism.

In view of the fact that in the 1950s the dominant nationalist leaders in most of the British colonies in the Caribbean area adopted policies of collaboration with imperialism,[112] it will perhaps be helpful at this point to explain the theoretical justifications of the Marxist-Leninist concept of the anti-imperialist front in the late 1930s. This can best be understood by looking at the strategy pursued by British imperialism prior to World War I. At that time it was the British Government's policy to retain the colonial relationship and use it so as to prevent or restrict the establishment of local industries which would compete with goods manufactured in Britain and exported to the colonies. Britain's effective control of colonial governments also enabled them to restrict and discourage penetration of their colonial markets by rival manufacturers in other developed countries.

The frustrated intelligentsia — those educated persons excluded by the system from access to the top administrative and managerial posts were becoming increasingly vocal in their support for national self determination. But the natural consequence of the implementation of imperialist economic policy was to make anti-imperialist ideas more acceptable also to persons in the colonies who wished to invest in local industries and to merchants who wished to have less restrictions on trade. Thus it transpired that some aspiring capitalists and merchants were willing to join in the demand for the right to form a government responsive to local rather than imperial interests. In the late 1930s, and indeed throughout the 1940s, there was a fertile soil in Jamaica for the cultivation of a broad anti-imperialist front. Not until a weakened Britain, no longer able to hold its empire together, initiated decolonisation and abandoned the policy of restricting local industrialisation, was the possibility of maintaining a broad anti-imperialist front undermined.[113]

The P.N.P. was launched at the Ward Theatre in Kingston in September 1938. Bustamante was prominently seated on the platform but was not invited to speak. The principal speakers were Norman Manley and Sir Stafford Cripps, the British Labour MP who happened at that time to be holidaying on the island. Subsequently, at the invitation of the Metropolitan Group of the party, Bustamante became, through that group, a member. But he never played an active part in the affairs of the P.N.P.

At that time Bustamante had no reason to believe that the British would be willing to alter the constitution of Jamaica and he may have regarded party politics as a waste of time. He must have realised that leading members of the party did not approve of the undemocratic constitution of his union, but as P.N.P. members were supporting the new trade union movement that he was leading and seldom if ever criticised him publicly he should not have had much cause for concern. Nevertheless, he did not welcome the idea of anyone else becoming popular with the masses and, if only for that reason, viewed the P.N.P. and particularly its leader, as a potential rival. His relationship with the party was therefore fluid and unpredictable. Sometimes he blew cold and encouraged his followers to disrupt P.N.P. street meetings. One way in which they did this was by drowning out the speakers with the singing of 'God Save the King'. Sometimes he blew hot and spoke favourably of his famous cousin. At a meeting of longshoremen in Kingston in February 1940 he was reported as saying that he was 'going to join up with Manley and change the government of this country'.[114]

Outside Union office — later in 1938.

Thirty-Nine

The Role Of The Marxist Left

There was one problem arising out of the decision to form a single multi-class party which had to be faced by the Marxist left. As Marxists we were committed to the concept that the working class is the principal instrument of social change and that only the working class, guided by Marxist-Leninist theory, can ultimately be relied upon to effect the transition from capitalism to socialism. Though we were convinced that this transition was not on the immediate agenda, there was an obvious danger of the left becoming absorbed in the broader organisation to the point of losing its identity and its ability to work out the correct strategy and tactics to be applied in an on-going and developing situation. It was important that Marxist-Leninist theory, which had been proved internationally to be a reliable guide for the working class, should not become diluted or distorted in practice in Jamaica by purely pragmatic and opportunistic considerations.

To meet this problem it was decided to preserve the identity of the Marxist left within the new party. Members of the Marxist left played a leading part in organising P.N.P. groups all over the country but we nevertheless maintained our own organisations within the party. The main organisation of the left was the Negro Workers Educational League which was formally affiliated to the party. In addition to this there was the somewhat ill-defined 'Inner Circle' of leading comrades, designed to co-ordinate and guide the work of the left within the party and the trade union movement.[115]

Among the outstanding contributions of the left to the early development of the P.N.P. two are deserving of special mention. The first was the achievement of bringing the nationalistic message of the party to the working class. Indeed, there were areas in western Kingston and western St. Andrew which 'respectable' middle class members of the party did not dare or care to visit, where the only public meetings at which the call for self government could be heard were those organised under the red flag of our Negro Workers Educational League. In these areas only the left spoke in terms which evoked a favourable response from the people.

The left also influenced the entire thinking of the party during the first decade of its existence in determining the content of its nationalism. The Marxist thesis was that the Crown Colony system was being maintained because it was the most effective political super-structure for exploitation of the resources and peoples of the colonies by the British capitalists. By explaining the connection between economic exploitation by foreign capital and the role of the colonial state, we were able to convince all strata of the party that the demand for self determination was based on something more substantial than an emotional quest for national prestige. Self government, we argued, could provide the opportunity for the economic development of our resources for the benefit of the people. And because our Marxist analysis made good sense not only to the workers but also to other strata, including nationalistic elements among the bourgeoisie and petty bourgeoisie, we were able to ensure that the nationalism of the P.N.P. was not narrowly anti-colonialist but also, in the broader economic and political sense, anti-imperialist.

Air base (Public Workers' Department) Workers' strike, May 1938.

Jamaica Labour
Weekly Attacked

he *Jamaica Labour Weekly,* though small in size, had become a very
opular voice of the workers. I do not think the number of copies prin-
d was very large, perhaps no more than a couple of thousands, but it
as being widely distributed throughout the island, through the local
rganisers of the Bustamante Union and also the surviving branches of
e Jamaica Workers and Tradesmen's Union. Not surprisingly
erefore it attracted the attention of the Colonial Government, and
as regarded by the establishment as an undersirable influence.

In the latter part of July 1938 the Colonial Government went onto
e offensive against the *Jamaica Labour Weekly.* Buchanan and Sten-
et Coombs, the printer, were prosecuted for seditious libel. The
arge was in connection with the article headlined 'Police Terror in St.
mes' published in the June 18 issue of the paper. The original story,
nt in by A.G.S. Coombs, had been an even stronger condemnation of
utal actions by the Special Constables, but Buchanan had toned it
wn somewhat before publication. Even so, it was enough to give the
overment the opportunity they wanted to silence the paper. Follow-
g the Preliminary Enquiry on August 30, Buchanan and Coombs were
mmitted for trial in the High Court.

The trial took place on October 4. The defendants were represen-
d by Norman Manley, instructed by Union solicitor Ross Livingston.
oth were found guilty and, subsequently, sentenced to imprisonment
r six months. They were imprisoned in Spanish Town. As a result the
ice of the *Jamaica Labour Weekly* was temporarily silenced.

I had gone to the country in September 1938 to concentrate on
udies for my intermediate examination and was at Mavis Bank when
e news came that Buchanan and Coombs had been sentenced to
ison. Wellesley McBean wrote me to say that he had been allowed to
sit Buchanan on October 25 and that Buchanan had asked that we

123

keep the paper going. He could not manage to do this without help bu lest I should think of rushing back to Kingston, he gave me some reali tic advice: 'I suggest that you put in all the effort you can muster now o your exam and in . . . time we can map out some definite arrangement . . with regard to the paper'.[116]

I returned to Kingston to sit the exam in November and at the end that month we began to make arrangements to restart the paper. I mu have approached Stennet Coombs on the matter because on Decembe 6 he wrote me to say that he had considered my proposal but ha decided to make no further publication until he was released. Coomb was the owner of the press and I suppose that if our respect for th rights of private property had been greater, we would have let it go that. However, we decided to go ahead with our plans. In the secon week of December we put out the leaflet headed 'Watch for the Retur of the Jamaica Labour Weekly', with this telling quotation from th issue of July 23:

> We knew that if our paper was to tell the truth to the world we woul incur the wrath of the capitalists and their government and th organised church.

The wrath of the government had been reflected in the impriso ment of the editor and printer, but the wrath of the church had also de cended upon the paper. I recall a vitriolic attack on the paper by a English clergyman stationed in the island, who was incensed by th biblical quotations.

On December 17, 1938 the paper reappeared on the streets. W were able to continue publication until the release of Buchanan an Coombs in April 1939. Every afternoon I would leave my office at fo o'clock and make my way up Johns Lane to the printery to do the edi ing. The articles and news items were written by McBean, Albreat Morris, Frank Hill and myself, with occasional help from Henry Fowl and others. Frank was, however, extremely busy at that time, as Fai clough and H.P. Jacobs had taken employment with the *Jamaica Sta dard* and he was editing and doing most of the writing of *Public Opinio* on his own.

On April 3,1939 Buchanan and Coombs were released from priso Sad to relate, though they had not been allowed to see each other, the had managed to quarrel in an exhange of correspondence. There is r record of what their disagreement was about, but it was serious enoug

124

destroy the possibility of the paper being carried on as before after their release. The last issue of the *Jamaica Labour Weekly* in which our group had any in-put was published on April 15, 1939. All subsequent issues of the paper, which continued for another three months, were produced by Coombs alone. In May the group printed a leaflet formally disassociating all the former contributors from the paper. The leaflet stated: 'S. Kerr Coombs, former comrade of Buchanan, has deviated from the principles for which the Labour Weekly stood'.[117] Symbolically at about this time, the frontispiece of the paper disappeared from the printery. Thus ended the first chapter of left labour journalism in Jamaica.

This same leaflet informed the reader that 'arrangements are being made to produce another paper which will carry on the old traditions of the *Labour Weekly*', but it was not until November 1939 that this promise was fulfilled with the launching of a weekly, *The Worker,* edited by Arthur Henry. In February 1940 *The Worker* became an afternoon daily paper edited in fact by Frank Hill, but it proved impossible to sustain it. In April 1940 its place was taken by the monthly *Worker and Peasant* edited by Arthur Henry. By then war time police censorship had been introduced and this was so severely applied that it became impossible to continue publication.

Forty-One

Labour Movement Jeopardized

During the second half of 1938 and the early part of 1939 the Bustamante Union expanded rapidly throughout most parts of the island. Most of the local leaders of the Jamaica Workers and Tradesmen's Union transferred their allegiance to the new trade union movement, but the parish of St. James was the exception. That was the area in which the Jamaica Workers and Tradesmen's Union, under the personal leadership of its President, A.G.S. Coombs, was most strongly entrenched. Bustamante, however, could not be persuaded to work with Coombs and was determined to dislodge him from his last stronghold. Coombs was still giving his support to the *Jamaica Labour Weekly* and our group was very much in favour of working class unity, but nothing that Buchanan could say to Bustamante on the subject had any effect.

In the second week of February 1939 Bustamante launched his campaign to win the leadership of the workers of St. James away from Coombs. St. William Grant, who had been employed as a union organiser, was sent ahead to Montego Bay to start the ball rolling. On Sunday June 12 Grant led a procession in the town. When he and his supporters reached Railway Lane he met a man named Reid, a member of the Jamaica Workers and Tradesmen's Union employed by the United Fruit Company as a boatman. Reid told Grant that the Bustamante Union was not wanted there and an altercation developed in which threats and counter-threats were made. Grant then telegraphed his head office reporting the incident. On the following Monday morning Bustamante arrived in Montego Bay and demanded the dismissal or suspension of Reid. Coombs, however, demanded that Reid be allowed to continue working and this the Company agreed to do. Bustamante then called on the workers on all three wharves in Montego Bay to strike. Work continued at the United Fruit Company wharf but

ased at the Standard Fruit Company and Jamaica Banana Producers
arves as these companies diverted the fruit from their collection
ints to Kingston by rail instead of bringing it to Montego Bay.[118]

During the course of an angry scene on one of the wharves, Bus-
mante had an altercation with C.B. Chambers, an officer of the
W.T.U. and alleged that the latter had personally insulted him. Bus-
mante then called for an all-island general strike of waterfront
rkers. This extraordinary and erratic behaviour on Bustamante's
rt in calling for an all-island strike on such a flimsy pretext, without
y proper preparation or consultation with the workers, created con-
erable embarrassment.

There were, indeed, a number of issues affecting the waterfront
rkers which required resolution. There had been a strike in Kingston
er the laying off of seven men working on the 'Lady Rodney' which
d been called off on January 4 on the understanding that the dispute
uld be submitted to arbitration, but more than five weeks had elap-
d and the Government had taken no steps to set up an arbitration
ard. There was also the important problem of representational rights
clearly it was necessary, in the interests of the waterfront workers,
at they should all be in the same union. This would have been the only
y to ensure that when there was a dispute in one port the shippers
uld be unable to defeat the workers by transferring the ship to
other port. It would therefore have made good sense for the Bus-
mante Union to have demanded sole bargaining rights for all water-
nt workers and a closed shop. Probably the employers would have
sisted this demand and, if the great majority of the workers were in
vour of such action, an all-island strike might eventually have been
e best course to adopt. But although real issues such as these were in
e background, these were not the reasons which had led to Bus-
mante's arbitrary call for a general waterfront workers strike, without
nsultation or preparation.

Faced with the 'fait accompli', the *Jamaica Labour Weekly,* in its
ue of February 18, 1939, had no alternative but to express support for
e strike and seek to bring the issues which would be of real concern to
e workers to the fore. Needless to say, we did so with considerable
barrassment, knowing the reasons why Bustamante had lost his
mper and embarked on this irresponsible and adventurist course.

The immediate reaction of the Government was to declare a state of
ergency and mobilise the local forces and Special Constables. Not

127

surprisingly, the response of the workers to the strike call had bee weak and it was a complete failure. Many workers who had responde to the call were victimised. This ill-considered move undoubted damaged Bustamante's reputation in the eyes of many workers in parts of the island and jeopardized the whole future of the new tra union movement.

Throughout the island the workers responded with enthusiasm to the news that peace and harmony had been established between Bustamante and A.G.S. Coombs, the two principal labour leaders, and the trade unions which they represented. Both men being nominally members of the Peoples National Party, readily agreed that the party should sponsor a meeting of public reconciliation. The meeting accordingly took place at the Kingston Race Course on February 25, 1939, at which the principal speakers were Bustamante, Coombs and N.W. Manley. It was reported in glowing terms in the *Jamaica Standard:*

> A historic scene was witnessed . . . when before thousands of labourers, shouting themselves hoarse, the union of Jamaica's two rival labour chiefs, Alexander Bustamante and A.G.S. Coombs was at long last accomplished as they shook hands, embraced warmly, and pledged themselves to fight together and as never before in the cause of labour.

Coombs was generous in his praise of Bustamante:

> One has sprung up among us in the person of Alexander Bustamante, one who . . . has done more for labour in this island than any other man. Those interested in the working population . . . must realise that labour is larger than the individual; therefore it is necessary to sink personal differences for the common good of all concerned.

Bustamante was less generous, expressing no recognition of the work that Coombs had done for labour. But he did speak in favour of unity: 'The reason why Mr. Coombs is here', he was reported to have said, 'is not because I personally need him, but because it was necessary for all branches, all leaders of Labour to unite for the good of Jamaica'. Manley, in his speech, outlined the objectives of the Trade Union Advisory Council and read what was described as 'a provisional constitution'.[120]

After a period of three weeks the Trade Union Advisory Council acquired a permanent secretary in the person of F.A. Glasspole. It would have been quite impossible for me to continue to perform the secretarial tasks while studying for my final examination. The Council also acquired a new chairman, N.N. Nethersole, and was later re-named the 'Trade Union Council', the individual members being replaced by representatives of the affiliated unions.

Forty-Three

Demand For Union Democratisation

One of the repercussions of the abortive strike called by Bustamante in February was that in March a group of union members, taking Bustamante up on his promise that the Union would be democratised, put forward some concrete criticisms and proposals. Their spokesman was Lionel Lynch, a member of our Marxist group, who had been appointed organiser for Portland. Lynch's letter to Bustamante, dated March 14, 1939, deplored the absence of proper records of union decisions and activities and complained that 'The B.I.T.U. is content to make the newspapers its minute books'. It is also called for the election of officers.

What happened next was explained to the *Gleaner* by a spokesman for the group, who may indeed have been Lynch himself although his name is not mentioned in the story which was published on March 31:

> Six days after our intention was published, a meeting was called at Edelweiss Park and Mr. Bustamante inflamed the meeting against us, calling us tools of the capitalists. The result was that we were not able to explain to the meeting what our intentions really were.

The spokesman added that 'Mr. Bustamante was annoyed because we sent the letter asking for reorganization to the T.U.C. Yet we wrote him asking him to receive a deputation . . . and up to now we have had no answer'. The spokesman then detailed their proposals:

(1) That there should be regular scheduled business meetings of each Group.

(2) That there should be a President, Vice President, Secretary, Assistant Secretary, Treasurer and managing committee of each union.

(3)   That the paid officers should be appointed by the Executive Committee of the Unions and that the Managing Committee should be elected by the Unionists from among the Unionists themselves.

(4)   That there should be an Executive Council elected by the members themselves.

These men argued, the report continued. 'that they were prepared to suffer pain and even death in the cause of improved conditions for Labour, but not ignorantly nor to suit anyone's ambition'.[121]

The truce between Bustamante and Coombs had not solved all the problems of a divided labour movement, but it was a step in the right direction. If we take the waterfront workers as an example we can see that more than a mere peace treaty between the leaders was required to achieve a permanent solution. It would obviously have been in the interests of the waterfront workers for them all to be in one and the same trade union, but to achieve this would have required agreement between all the unions on a national structure for the trade union movement. Ideally what was required was a unity conference, with the participation of workers delegations from the various industries to work out an all-island plan for the structure of the trade union movement and a clear understanding as to which union would organise the workers in which industry or occupation. As the B.I.T.U. the J.W.T.U. and other unions, such as the shop assistants' J.U.C.A. and the Builders and Allied Trade Union, were all members of the Trade Union Advisory Council, such a conference might well have been organised under its auspices.

Any such democratic solution of the problem of labour disunity would, however, have run directly contrary to Bustamante's proprietory concept of trade unionism. It is not unreasonable to suppose that Bustamante had from the start regarded his truce with Coombs as a temporary expedient and that he had entered into it in February 1939 merely to safeguard himself against the probability of imprisonment following the call he had so impulsively made for a general strike. It is therefore not surprising that Bustamante should have withdrawn from the Trades Union Advisory Council and abandoned the agreement as soon as he felt that he was no longer threatened by the possibility of imprisonment under the state of emergency. He then reverted to his own way of achieving unification under his personal control — the destruction of all other organisations.

This renewal of internecine strife and Bustamante's contempt for democracy dampened the hopes of a united labour movement which had flourished at the time of the formation of the Trades Union Advisory Council. Bustamante's withdrawal from the T.U.A.C. was followed by the hiving off from his union of the public passenger transport workers, who set up their own union. The inaugural meeting of this union, the Tramway Transport and General Workers Union, was held at 124 Orange Street in a hall appropriately known as Union Hall on May 23, 1939. It was held at midnight, when all the tram and motor omnibus workers were off duty. The person these workers chose for their President was Ken Hill, who had originally led the bus drivers into the Bustamante fold but now resigned as Vice President of the B.I.T.U. Though the process went no further at this time, the hiving off of workers in various industries and occupations to form their own unions developed a real momentum in 1942 and the unions so formed affiliated to the Trades Union Council. But that is another story which is outside the scope of this review.

Another serious reversal to the prospects of transforming the B.I.T.U. from within came at this time when Buchanan lost his post as General Secretary. Why Bustamante should have decided to remove him and when it was that he decided to do so is not recorded. Obviously concern would have been felt in official quarters that the leader of the Marxist group held such an important position. Whether this in any way influenced Bustamante is not known, but sooner or later his own conservatism and businessman's approach to trade unionism would have caused him to develop similar concerns. Be that as it may, when Buchanan was released from prison on April 3 he was not reinstated as General Secretary but was assigned to lesser duties. J.A.G. Edwards, who had been appointed to act in his absence, was confirmed in the post.

Yet another consequence of the weakening of the labour movement, caused by Bustamante's proprietory approach and the disunity which ensued, was that it emboldened some of the principal shipping interests to give encouragement to a strike-breaking organisation of former members of the armed forces, the Jamaica Ex-Servicemen's Union led by H.M. Reid, a former soldier in the British West India Regiment. At the same time it encouraged the Government to make an attempt to undermine established wage rates by offering 'relief' work to unemployed workers at less than half the daily rate for labour as agreed during the previous year before the Conciliation Board. Instead of the standard daily rate of 3/9d [37½¢] the relief workers were offered 1/6d [15¢]. These two issues came to a climax in June 1939 and became inextricably linked.

Matters came to a head on June 16 when a large crowd attacked the headquarters of the Ex-Servicemen's Union and was alleged to have attempted to set it on fire. Police opened fire on the crowd, which retaliated with a barrage of stones and four policemen were taken to hospital. The Government responded next day by mobilising its military forces and four hundred Special Constables. A Reuters News Agency cable stated that 'Stones were thrown and lamps smashed in an hour long battle in Kingston's main thoroughfare' and that the cause was 'the terms of the Government's offer of relief work'.

June 18 was a Sunday and arrangements had been made to employ members of the Ex-Servicemen's Union at No. 2 Pier in Kingston. A police party was escorting these men to work at 7.30 a.m. when, according to the police report, they were attacked by a crowd which they estimated at six hundred. The police again opened fire, 'in self defence' according to the Governor, and as a result one man was mortally wounded and died in Hospital.[122] That man, according to the *London Times* report of the incident, 'was not one of the rioters'.[123]

In a long telegram to the Secretary of State for the Colonies, the Governor indicated that the two issues were related. Endeavouring to explain what had occurred, he said:

> I attribute the cause of the outbreak of discord to
>
> (a) Misunderstanding which has been deliberately and maliciously fostered by certain elements in print and speeches that the Government Unemployment Relief programme is an attempt to reduce ordinary wages . . .
>
> (b) Dissension among the Unions of their followers.
>
> (c) Presence in Kingston of hooligan and criminal element which is always ready to take advantage of any unrest.

He went on to say that he considered it 'essential that street meetings should be prohibited during times of tension' and to announce the introduction of a Bill for prohibiting meetings and processions.[124]

The Governor's comment about a 'misunderstanding' of the relief works programme being fostered 'in print and speeches', may have been a reference to the Jamaica Unemployed League, launched shortly before these events by our group with Buchanan as Secretary. This organisation, during the short period of its existence, issued a number of leaflets attacking the Government's attempt to undermine the level of wages and demanding that relief workers be paid at the full Conciliation Board rate of three shillings and nine pence per day. As a result of this agitation the Government was forced to increase the pay of the relief workers to 2/- (20¢) for a reduced working day of six hours.

Police clearing crowd from Church Street, May 23rd 1938.

Forty-Four

Buchanan's Open Letter To Bustamante

Finding himself in conflict with Bustamante over the way the Union's affairs were being conducted and being powerless to do anything about it, Buchanan eventually resigned. He set out his criticisms in an open letter to Bustamante, which was published in *The Worker* on December 22, 1939:

Dear Bustamante,

I am sorry that what I am going to say to you cannot be said at a properly constituted Executive or Members meeting. You accuse me of not being a member of the Union. But what is the use of joining and paying my money weekly when I will be kicked out and threatened with mob violence if I dare to ask any questions? Believe me that I would be one of the most active and loyal members of the Union if there was any protection or encouragement of free speech. In the absence of any such protection, I am forced to speak from the outside. This I do much to my regret, because speaking from the outside makes one appear so much like an enemy in the eyes of a certain section of the workers. Besides, an open discussion in the press must do the Union some hurt as confidence will gradually diminish.

However, the responsibility is yours — doubly yours, because apart from having blundered hopelessly, you effectively closed all the avenues of free speech within the Union.

You may ask — What interest have I that although being not a paying member I continue to interfere? I answer — my approach to the Union movement is different from yours. You have repeatedly said you are a rich man, you need no union for yourself, you are only doing what you do out of sympathy for us. As a workman who has to approach the pay table for a living, I need a union. When the Union is strong, I am strong, I can look forward to each succeeding day with greater confidence. That is why I will not leave things alone, I am no sympathizer, my interests are directly threatened.

If work in building up a labour sentiment counts for anything, I can claim to have done my bit. And if anyone doubted my sincerity, I stood six months imprisonment, without quailing. This, I admit, is somewhat individualistic; but it is only a prelude to establish my right to say what I have to tell you. Otherwise you might be tempted to rule out my case and I am determined that you shall not.

When the workers struck last year May, that was their own effort. No one man can take any credit for it. You got arrested in the course of the struggle and we did not leave you in the lurch, we stood behind you like a rock. Had we urged the men at the waterfront to go back to work before you were released, they would have gone back and you would go to prison. Knowing the game, we stood firm even at the peril of our own liberty. In that crisis to get you out of jail before any going back to work, I was one of the desperately resolute.

While defending you, I had not forgotten the mean dirty trick you played in the Jamaica Workers and Tradesmen's Union which smashed it to pieces. You will remember I was General Secretary of the Union at that time and I know everything. But the people had proclaimed you as their leader, an avalanche was rolling and we were carried down with it.

When the tumult of the first wave of strikes died down the workers demanded to be organised in unions. They knew that some organization was necessary to hold whatever little gains they had won, and to battle for further concessions. After some delay you started enrolment and members poured in by tens of thousands. Some Branches started to collect dues and send it to Union Headquarters even without authority. Today, what is the position?

The most flourishing Branches are dead, and the Union possesses but a shadow of its former power if any at all. Discontent is rampant, but you just ignore it, or brand those who are brave enough to raise their voices as traitors. Consequently you are engaged in a permanent traitor-hunting and denouncing campaign. While you are busy hunting and denouncing your imaginary traitors, nothing is being done for the workers. Conditions are now almost worse than they were before the strike last year.

The Longshoremen were the most resolute workers last May. They formed the most solid block in the Union, today they are in slavery again. Reid's strike breaking Union has got a stranglehold upon the waterfront and is threatening to extend its operations. The victimised longshoremen are left to perish. You have refused to arbitrate their case on the grounds that you were waiting for the Labour Adviser. The Labour Adviser is here since July. What have you done about it? Nothing.

Have you forgotten the Sanitary men of the KSAC? Last year May they played their part. Today, they are being forced to sign a contract to do away with their pensions and gratuities. What are you doing about it?

As a result of the war, prices of all articles consumed by the workers have increased considerably. Rent is also being pushed up. Newspaper reports carry increases of salary being negotiated for and obtained by the Unions in England. When are you going to make a move for the members of your Union?

To do any of these things, it is obvious that you must have a strong Union. A strong Union can only be made through the confidence of the members in the leadership. Unfortunately, things have come to such a pass where confidence has disappeared. From the time of that strike in February, if you had taken warning the position would have been different today. But you recklessly plunged along in the same course, and you seriously endangered the life of the Union.

Even at this late hour, it is possible for you to recover lost ground; because the workers are in a mood to organise. Economic pressure is getting tighter and tighter. They have tasted of the good fruits of militant unity and have not forgotten it yet. All that is wanted to do the job is Confidence. The workers have already done their part by joining in large numbers and paying their money. Everybody knows what happened.

In order to restore confidence you must make the next move. The first step I suggest is to scrap the Constitution: it is the most fraudulent thing ever printed. the new Constitution should get the approval of the membership before it is registered. However good a Constitution you will make, it is quite possible for you to disregard it and continue being the Dictator that you are now. You must therefore be prepared to give up some of your one-man power and take the officers and members into partnership.

I consider it unfortunate under our circumstances that so many Industries and Trades should be lumped in one union. The original plan separate Industrial Unions should not have been abandoned. All you had to do was to elect proper officers and have the Unions well scrutinized. Seeing that the membership of all the possible Industrial Unions combined may not exceed 100,000, a blanket union properly sectionized and staffed ought to achieve high degree of efficiency.

These suggestions if put into effect will kill all the plotters and traitors. When there are any differences it will be thrashed within the Union and not become a public scandal. Take my advice and adopt these suggestions and the Union will start to live again.[125]

Outside Manley's chambers during 1946 Government workers' strikes.

Forty-Five

The P.N.P.'s First Conference

The first Annual Conference of the People's National Party was held in Kingston from April 12 to 14, 1939. The Policy and Programme approved at that conference contained the following proposal for constitutional advancement:

> The Party advocates and will work to achieve the claim of this country to a representative form of Government as a Unit of the British Commonwealth of Nations. The system advocated is that of a parliamentary democracy on the lines which obtain in other self governing units of the British Commonwealth . . . The Party advocates and supports the right of all persons of full age and without disability to a vote as a condition precedent to a representative form of Government.

Under the heading 'Industrial Development' the statement declared:

> The Party Policy advocates the encouragement and development of local industries both agricultural and otherwise as an essential feature of the development of the country's productivity and resources. The Programme recommends the institution of Statutory Industries Boards supported by adequate legislative power for the safe-guarding and protection of local Industries.
>
> The Industrial programme of the Party advocates:
>
> (a) The public ownership of all industries which enjoy a complete monopoly.
>
> (b) The public ownership or effective state control of all industries which enjoy or require subsidies from public funds.
>
> (c) The State ownership of all public utilities.[126]

It will be observed that, in its advocacy of 'a parliamentary democracy on the lines which obtain in other self-governing units of the British Commonwealth', the party had already made an advance on the position which Norman Manley had adopted before the Royal Commission in November 1938, when he said that self-government should not be granted immediately. Manley was fully in support of the party's April 1939 declaration.

However, when Britain declared war on Germany in September 1939 and launched what came to be known as 'the phoney war', Manley persuaded the Executive Committee of the P.N.P. to suspend agitation for self-government for the duration of the War. This decision, though largely ignored in practice, was not formally reversed until the party's Second Annual Conference on August 28, 1940.[127]

Forty-Six

Manley's Relations With 'Communists'

Yet another contemporary letter which deserves a place in this survey of the popular awakening over the period from 1936 to 1939, if only because it illustrates so well the relationship between the Marxist left and the dominant middle class section of the national movement, is a letter which I wrote to Norman Manley on December 29, 1939. The context in which the letter was written was that the P.N.P. was endeavouring to make a political breakthrough in a K.S.A.C. by-election in a constituency in which middle class voters were numerous, at a time when the franchise was still restricted to about ten per cent of the adult population. This letter, reproduced below, will facilitate an understanding of the contemporary scene:

December 29th 1939

Dear Mr. Manley,

I am taking this opportunity of writing you fully in connection with the request you made to Frank Hill and myself that those openly acknowledging themselves as Communists should withdraw from participation on the platform in the Nethersole by-election campaign. We have considered the matter very carefully and are now willing to accede to your request, though I think you will agree that we took the wisest course in not coming to any rapid ill-considered decision on a matter of such far reaching importance.

You will readily understand our fears that this may be, to use your own words, 'the thin edge of the wedge' in an effort which will inevitably be made by a certain element to deny Communists the right to participate in our national movement. This move will come, no matter how much you personally disapprove of it, but it is certainly reassuring to know that if and when it comes you will resist it.

144

This situation is not without parallel in recent history. I would bring to your attention the manner in which the Chinese National Kuomintang Party was purged of Communists in 1927 by the reactionary general Chiang Kai Chek. The tremendous struggle waged by the Chinese Communists for the formation of a united front against the common enemy has at last borne fruit, but even so their position is by no means secure. Of course the Communists in Jamaica are not organised in a militant mass party, but the similarity of our role will become more apparent as the consciousness of the toiling masses develops.

As against these considerations, therefore, it was necessary for us to weigh the effects of our participation in the present by-election campaign. You argue that we will lessen the P.N.P. candidate's chances by appearing on his platform. And we are of the opinion that such work as we have done for the Party on the platform has had the reverse effect to date. A very similar situation arose when the British Communists supported Herbert Morrison in the L.C.C. elections contrary to the wishes of the executive of the Labour Party.

However, in view of the immediate importance of Nethersole's success and your fears that as the time draws near the Communist bogey will be used more effectively by his opponents, we are willing to fall in with your suggestion and take no further part in this by-election.

Yours fraternally
A. Richard Hart [128]

Forty-Seven

The Anti-Imperialist Stage

It may be helpful, finally, to discuss the theoretical principles which guided Jamaican Marxists in the late 1930s. These may be summarised as follows:

1.   A socialist economic system involving public ownership of the principal means of production and distribution would more effectively meet the material and cultural needs of our people than the existing capitalist-imperialist system.

2.   There was much to be learned from studying the experiences of other peoples, but the transition from capitalism to socialism in Jamaica could proceed only in the manner and by the stages appropriate to Jamaican conditions.

3.   Having regard to the social composition of Jamaica and its economic under-development, the first stage in our transition had to be a struggle to free Jamaica from the economic exploitation and political control of British imperialism.

4.   To struggle effectively against British imperialism it was necessary to mobilise the social strata oppressed or impeded by imperialism.

5.   To this end it was necessary to forge a political alliance between representatives of the workers and peasants, the self-employed artisans, the small businessmen and shopkeepers and the professional and administrative middle class.

6.   The best form for such an alliance to take would be a single political party within which the Marxist left, representing working class interests, would preserve its separate identity while participating fully in building up support for the party among all social strata.

How did Jamaican Marxists arrive at these theoretical conclusions? Though Marx had condemned the oppression of other nations by developed capitalist states (for example, British rule in India and Ireland), there was nothing to be found in his writings regarding the formation of an anti-imperialist front in a colonial or semi-colonial country. It could not have been otherwise because Marx had died before capitalism had developed into the monopoly stage which had created the conditions for modern imperialism. It was the emergence at the turn of the century of the capitalist monopolies of western Europe and North America, with their massive accumulations of capital available for overseas investment and their tremendous productive capacities seeking overseas markets, which had led to the parcelling out of the greater part of the under-developed world and ushered in the era of modern imperialism.

So it was Lenin who, after Marx's death but using his method of historical analysis, made a special study of capitalism in its imperialist stage. It was Lenin who worked out the broad theoretical principles for the anti-imperialist struggle of the oppressed peoples in the colonial and semi-colonial countries.

Lenin did not have things all his own way. At the congresses of the Communist International in the early 1920s he had had to combat the impatience of Marxists from some of the colonial countries, notably M.N. Roy of India, who believed that the Russian Revolution, which had greatly inspired them, could be duplicated in their own countries. Lenin had also had to oppose certain adventurist views of members of his own party, notably those of Leon Trotsky and his followers. Lenin argued that the approach to socialism in each country required an analysis of its social structure and stage of development and that most colonial and semi-colonial peoples would first have to go through the stage of a struggle against imperialism, which the workers would have to wage jointly with other social strata.

Lenin's view had won acceptance at the Second Congress of the Communist International in 1920, though affiliated working class parties did not always follow the Communist International's advice. However, our Marxist group in Jamaica, formed in 1937, had no contacts with the Communist International and no knowledge of these debates on a matter which was obviously of great concern to us. Our earliest Marxist contacts abroad were with Domingo and O'Meally in New York, neither of whom had ever been a member of the Communist

Party of the U.S.A. Nor did our subsequent contacts with the British Communists help to enlighten us.

We had of course posted copies of the *Jamaica Labour Weekly* to the British Communist Party, but apart from mentioning the paper and the imprisonment of its editor in their *Colonial Information Bulletin,* they had shown no interest in us. Our first contact with British Communists had come, quite by chance, towards the end of 1938 when Harry Pollit, its General Secretary, came to Jamaica on a Caribbean cruise. Suffering from a severe illness, Pollit's doctor had prescribed relaxation in a warm climate and his comrades had carried him abroad a cruise ship on a stretcher. By the time he had reached Jamaica he had recuperated sufficiently to pay a visit to Bustamante and it was in Bustamante's office that I met him.

Pollit put us in touch with Ben Bradley, who was running the British C.P.'s Colonial Information Bureau and we began to correspond. But although the British C.P. was then affiliated to the Communist International, it never seems to have occurred to them to send us copies of its debates or statements. A letter from Bradley in July 1939 mentioned that, in addition to the *Jamaica Labour Weekly,* I had sent him a letter and press cuttings which he found 'extremely interesting', but we received no comments whatsoever which would have contributed to our knowledge of Marxist theory in relation to the anti-imperialist struggle. Indeed, I cannot recall any assistance from the British C.P. during our formative period. If anything, it was the other way, in the form of information about our struggles for their publications.

My letters to the late Ben Bradley probably contained some interesting information on the situation in Jamaica in 1939, but unfortunately copies were not preserved. The Librarian at the British Communist Party Headquarters kindly allowed me to look for the letters in the Bradley papers, but all these related to the famous Meerut conspiracy trial in India, in which Bradley was a defendant. My letters were not there, but I did find evidence of something I had sent. The quotation from the *Jamaica Standard* story of the meeting at the Kingston Race Course on February 25, 1939, had been reprinted in their *Colonial Information Bulletin.*

During 1938, when Jamaican Marxists were analysing the class structure, degree of under-development and imperialist exploitation and political realities of the island and endeavouring to apply Marxist theory to the local situation, very few copies of Marxist works were available in Jamaica. I can recall only one copy of each of Lenin's classic studies *Imperialism, the Highest Stage of Capitalism* and *The State and Revolution,* though we had several copies of *The Communist Manifesto* by Marx and Engels. Another important book of which I can recall there being only one copy, was *Marxism and the National and Colonial Question,* containing J.V. Stalin's excellent expositions of Marxist-Leninist theory on the formation of nations and the anti-imperialist struggle. We did attempt to overcome this problem by arranging for the last mentioned book to be reviewed and discussed at a meeting of the Left Book Club, but that was not until October 1939.

the Left Book Club, formed in 1938, shared premises in Kingston Gardens with the Readers and Writers Club and there was such an over-lapping of membership that the two organisations became almost indistinguishable. Our local Left Book Club was modelled on the Left Book Clubs formed in England in 1936 by an enterprising publisher, Victor Gollancz, through which he provided members with the opportunity to buy books by leftist authors very cheaply. The publishers were persuaded to appoint Wellesley McBean as distributing agent for the books. But whereas in England the Left Book Club was confined to persons who guaranteed to buy one book per month, our club in Jamaica was open to all who wanted to read the books or attend its meetings. This was the principal source of books by Marxist and other leftist authors in Jamaica at that time.

Despite the limitations referred to and the intellectual vacuum which was our educational inheritance as a British colony, Jamaican Marxists nevertheless succeeded in making a reasonably sound analysis of the economic situation and political realities of Jamaica in 1938. In retrospect it would appear that the conclusions we reached at that time, as to the form our anti-imperialist struggle should take, were probably correct.

References

1. K. Marx to F. Engels, April 9, 1863 in *Marx-Engels Selected Correspondence,* Progress Publishers, Moscow, 1975, p. 131.

2. R. Hart, *Origin & Development of the Working Class in the English-Speaking Caribbean Area — 1897 to 1937,* Community Education Trust, London n.d. (1984).

3. Local white or pass-white officials in Jamaica in the 1930s and early 1940s included W.H. Orrett, who headed the Islands Police Force, W.A. Orrett in charge of the Police in Kingston and St. Lucia born B.H. Easter, the Director of Education.

4. P.W. Gibson, former headmaster of Kingston College.

5. W.M. Macmillan, *Warning from the West Indies,* Penguin Books, London, 1938.

6. The first legislation permiting the formation of trade unions in Jamaica (1919) and British Guiana (1921) did not provide for peaceful picketing or grant unions immunity from actions in tort. When similar legislation was being enacted in Trinidad & Tobago in 1932-33, unsuccessful representations were made to the British Government for inclusion of peaceful picketing provisions. As a consequence of this similar legislation in Grenada, which had been delayed at T.A. Marryshow's request to await the outcome of the Trinidad representations, was also brought into force in 1934 without provision for peaceful picketing. (Public Record Office, London: CO 104/52 — Grenada Leg. Co. Minutes Nov. 15 and Dec. 29, 1933).

7. *Plain Talk,* Jan. 28, 1938, quoted in K. Post, *Arise Ye Starvelings,* Martinus Nijhoff, The Hague, 1978, p. 262 n. 21.

8. Information from Lester Hay, Buchanan's school mate, now residing in Birmingham, England.

9.   *Public Opinion* Dec. 18, 1937 — quoted in K. Post, *Arise Ye Starvelings,* pp. 5-6.

10.   Post, *Arise Ye Starvelings,* p. 350 citing *Jamaica Standard* May 13, 1938.

11.   The statement in Frank Hill, *Bustamante and his Letters,* Kingston Publishers, Kingston, 1976, that Buchanan had attended a meeting of the Communist International in Hamburg in the early 1930s is incorrect. There was a meeting of the Red International of Trade Unions (not the Communist International) in Hamburg in that year, but the persons from the English-speaking Caribbean area who attended were Hubert Critchlow (British Guiana), Vivian Henry (Trinidad) and S.M. DeLeon (Jamaica). DeLeon was one of the founders in 1929 of the short-lived Jamaica Trades & Labour Union and secretary of a committee formed by Marcus Garvey in 1930 'to pave the way for labour unions'. (*The Blackman,* April 26, 1930).

12.   *Public Opinion* July 3, 1937 — quoted in K. Post, *Arise Ye Starvelings,* p. 175.

13.   L. Lynch to R. Hart, May 21, 1985. Lynch died in Birmingham on June 15, 1985, aged 75.

14.   Some of the early Marxists were unable to stand the pressures and later dropped out of political activity. Others, who remained active politically and in the trade union movement, succumbed to opportunism and repudiated Marxism. These desertions did not, however, commence until after the period here under review.

15.   *Public Opinion* June 5, 1937, p. 3.

16.   *Eighth Census of Jamaica and its Dependencies, 1943,* Central Bureau of Statistics, Kingston, 1945, pp. 148, 169.

17.   *Eighth Census,* pp. XCV, 308.

18.   *Eighth Census,* p. XCVI.

19.   *Labour Department Annual Report, 1945* Kingston — quoted in T. Munroe, *The Marxist Left in Jamaica, 1940-1950,* Inst. of Social & Econ. Research, Univ. of the W.I., Mona, Ja., 1977, p. 10.

20.   PRO: C.O. 137/820 file 68857, Governor to Secretary of State, Sept. 21 and Nov. 2, 1937 — cited in K. Post *Arise Ye Starvelings,* p. 119.

21.   *Plain Talk* Nov. 2, 1935 — cited in K. Post, *Arise Ye Starvelings,* p. 246 — all subsequent quotes from *Plain Talk* are from this source.

22.   *Plain Talk* Aug. 5, 14 and Sept. 7, 1935.

23.   D. Reid and others, petition to Governor, in *Plain Talk,* Dec. 21, 1935.

24.   *Plain Talk* Dec. 28, 1935 — letter from D. Reid and others.

25.   *Plain Talk* Dec. 5, 1936 — letter from W.D. Walters on behalf of the Tax & Ratepayers Assn.

26.   R. Hill & R. Small, 'The Teaching of Robert E. Rumble, a Jamaican Peasant Leader' in *Education and Black Struggle,* Harvard Educ. Review monograph No. 2/1974, Cambridge, Mass.

27.   *Plain Talk* Feb. 20 and March 3, 1937.

28.   K. Post, *Arise Ye Starvelings,* p. 249.

29.   Petition published in *Plain Talk,* April 30, 1938.

30.   B. St.J Hamilton, *Bustamante, Anthology of a Hero,* Publishers & Producers, Kingston, 1977, contains probably the most careful attempt to unravel Bustamante's elusive earlier life and separate the facts from his subject's imaginative embellishments. Bustamante, incidentally, was Norman Manley's first cousin.

31.   PRO: C.O. 950/152, file J. 206 — Memorandum of Govt. of Ja. on unemployment and rates of wages.

32.   PRO: C.O. 950/185, file J. 246 — Memorandum of the Bustamante Industrial Trade Unions, 10 Nov. 1938.

33.   PRO: C.O. 950/144, file J. 195 — Memorandum of Walter Bethune.

34.   PRO: C.O. 950/86, file J. 182 — Evidence of A.G.S. Coombs for the Jamaica Workers & Tradesmen Union.

35.   Ibid — Evidence of G. Hawkins, manager and part owner of Tremolesworth plantation.

36.   *Report (with Appendices) of the Commission appointed to enquire into the Disturbances which occurred in Jamaica Between the 23rd May and the 8th June, 1938,* Govt. Printing Office, Kingston, 1938 — App. I

hereafter called 'All Island Disturbances Report').

37.   *Report (with Appendices) of the Commission appointed to enquire into Disturbances which occurred on Frome Estate in Westmoreland on 2nd May 1938,* Govt. Printing Office, Kingston 1938. (hereafter called Frome Report').

38.   *Daily Gleaner,* May 3, 1938.

39.   *Daily Gleaner,* May 4, 1938.

40.   *Daily Gleaner,* May 3, 1938.

41.   *Daily Gleaner* May 4, 1938.

42.   PRO: C.O. 140/293 — Ja. Privy Council Minutes, May 7, 1938.

43.   Frome Report.

44.   *Daily Gleaner,* May 19, 1938.

45.   *Daily Gleaner,* May 21 and 23, 1938.

46.   *Daily Gleaner,* May 23, 1938

47.   R. Hart to J. O'Meally, June 1, 1938.

48.   Ibid.

49.   My account written May 24, 1938 hereafter called "Hart Diary".

50.   *All Island Disturbances Report,* App. I, p. 5.

51.   Hart Diary.

52.   *All Island Disturbances Report,* App. I. p. 5.

53.   *All Island Disturbances Report,* App. I. p. 6.

54.   *All Island Disturbances Report,* App. I. p. 5.

55.   Ibid, App. I. p. 6.

56.   *Daily Gleaner,* May 25, 1938.

57.   Ibid.

58.   *All Island Disturbances Report,* App. I. p. 6.

59.   Quoted in Rex Nettleford (ed.) *Manley & the New Jamaica,* Longman Caribbean, London, 1971, pp. xlii-xliv. The rumour referred to was that, when requested by E.R.D. Evans, solicitor for the Jamaica

Progressive League, to accept a brief to defend the Frome strikers, he
had at first agreed to, then subsequently turned it down. (See the mention
of this misunderstanding in my letter on pp. 88-90).

60.   *Jamaica Journal* (Vol. 7. No. 1-2) March-June, 1973 — 'The
Autobiography of Norman Washington Manley'. In this memoir, which
he did not write until June 28, 1969, Manley stated that it was on the day
of his return to Kingston (May 23rd) that he spent the afternoon 'moving
around to see what the city looked like'. This would appear to be a
mistake as his diary records that he made his 'perambulation' on the
following day. This error is confirmed by the fact that he records the
arrest of Bustamante and Grant in the memoir and this did not occur
until May 24.

61.   *Daily Gleaner,* May 25,1938.

62.   Ibid.

63.   Ibid.

64.   *Daily Gleaner,* May 26, 1938.

65.   Ibid.

66.   Ibid.

67.   W.A. Williams had emerged during the strike as the longshoremen's leader. Bustamante subsequently made him a Vice President of the Union.

68.   *Jamaica Labour Weekly* May 28, 1938; *Daily Gleaner,* May
28, 1938.

69.   *All Island Disturbances Report,* App. I, pp. 6-7.

70.   *Daily Gleaner,* May 27, 1938.

71.   Ibid.

72.   *Daily Gleaner,* May 28, 1938.

73.   W.A. Domingo to R. Hart, May 27, 1938, acknowledging cable
and promising a prompt response. Responding to similar requests, the
British T.U.C. sent model constitutions to L.E. Barnett, organising
workers at Linstead, in 1937, and C.S. Maxwell, later Builder and Allied
T.U. Secretary, on May 26, 1938 (T.U.C. File 972. 1 Jamaica 1). For this
information I am indebted to Majorie Nicholson (letter August 9,
1985).

74.   *Daily Gleaner,* May 27, 1938.

75.   *All Island Disturbances Report,* App. I, p. 7.

76.   *Daily Gleaner,* May 27, 1938.

77.   Ibid.

78.   Ibid.

79.   *All Island Disturbances Report,* App. I, p. 7.

80.   *Daily Gleaner,* May 30, 1938; PRO: C.O. 140/293 — Jamaica Privy Council Minutes, June 6, 15, 1938.

81.   *All Island Disturbances Report,* App. I. p. 7.

82.   *Daily Gleaner,* May 30, 1938.

83.   Ibid.

84.   *Daily Gleaner,* May 31, 1938.

85.   *All Island Disturbances Report,* App. I. pp. 8-12.

86.   Ibid.

87.   *Daily Gleaner,* June 1, 1938.

88.   *All Island Disturbances Report,* App. I. pp. 8-12.

89.   Ibid.

90.   *Daily Gleaner,* June 2, 1938.

91.   *Daily Gleaner,* June 3, 1938.

92.   *Daily Gleaner,* June 4, 1938.

93.   *All Island Disturbances Report,* p. 14.

94.   Ibid, App. I, pp. 10-12.

95.   *Jamaica Standard,* May 25, 1938 — quoted in K. Post, *Arise Ye Starvelings,* p. 249.

96.   PRO: C.O. 137/827. File 68868/1 — Minute by J.H. Emmens, June 23, 1938.

97.   *Daily Gleaner,* December 28, 1938.

98.   *All Island Disturbances Report,* App. I, p. 11.

99.   *Daily Gleaner,* June 6, 1938.

100.   PRO: C.O. 137/827. File 68868/2 — Cabinet papers.

101.   *Daily Gleaner,* May 30, 1938.

102.   PRO: C.O. 950/185. File J. 246 — A note on this stationery is in this file.

103.   *Jamaica Labour Weekly,* July 9, 1938.

104.   PRO: C.O. 950/185. File J. 246.

105.   R. Hart to J. O'Meally, June 1, 1938.

106.   *Jamaica Labour Weekly,* May 21, 1938.

107.   W.A. Domingo to R. Hart, July 13, 1938.

108.   Jamaica Progressive League.

109.   A. Lozovsky, *Marx and the Trade Unions,* International Publishers, New York, 1935, pp. 15, 18.

110.   Articles relevant to this debate appeared in the issues of *Public Opinion* dated Dec. 24, 1937 (Roberts); Dec. 31 (ARH — the writer); Jan. 8, 1938 (Buchanan); Jan 22 (O'Meally); Feb. 12 (ARH); March 5 (Domingo); March 12 (O'Meally); March 19 (ARH); April 16 (W.A. McBean). The debate is reviewed in K. Post, *Arise Ye Starvelings,* pp. 226-31. Also of relevance is O.T. Fairclough's article 'The Jamaica Labour Party' in *Public Opinion,* May 28, 1938.

111.   PRO: C.O. 950/86. File J. 121 — Evidence of N.W. Manley and others before the W.I. Royal Commission.

112.   The first indication that this process was under way came with the appointment of Grantley Adams of Barbados as a member of the British Government's delegation to the United Nations General Assembly in 1948. Adams' role (a role T.A. Marryshow of Grenada declined to play despite his strong Anglophile sentiments) was to make the first speech by a colonial leader attacking the USSR and praising British colonial policies. In the following year Norman Manley for the first time advocated the policy of relying on direct investments of foreign capital to create new industries (the Puerto Rican model), though he did not get an opportunity to implement it by granting tax holidays to foreign investors until he became Premier in 1955.

113.   This whole question is considered in greater depth with examples of how the various social strata were impeded and frustrated, in my

paper on 'Jamaica and Self-Determination, 1660 to 1970' in *Race,* Vol. XIII No. 3 (1972).

114.   *The Worker,* Feb. 16, 1940.

115.   This structure whereby the left operated as a more or less disciplined group within the People's National Party was dissolved in 1944 when the existence of organised groups, other than ordinary P.N.P. Groups which anyone could join, was no longer permitted. How this came about and what happened afterwards is outside the scope of this review.

116.   W.A. McBean to R. Hart Oct. 31, 1938.

117.   *Jamaica Labour Weekly,* May 20, 1939.

118.   PRO: C.O. 137/836 — proceedings of the Legislative Council, Governor Richards' report to members on February 16, 1939.

119.   *Jamaica Labour Weekly,* February 25, 1939.

120.   *Jamaica Standard,* February 26, 1939 quoted in *Colonial Information Bulletin,* London, April 1, 1939.

121.   *Daily Gleaner,* March 31, 1939.

122.   PRO: C.O. 137/836. File 68868.

123.   *The Times,* London June 20, 1939.

124.   PRO: C.O. 137/836. File 68868.

125.   *The Worker,* Dec. 22, 1939, reprinted in *Socialism* (Vo.2, No. 5). May 1975.

126.   *Outline of the Policy and Programme of the People's National Party,* Kingston 1939. (Copy in the writer's collection of P.N.P. publications 1938-56 in the Jamaica Library, Inst. of Ja.

127.   *The Peoples National Party: Report of the 2nd Annual Conference,* Kingston, 1940.

128.   A.R. Hart to N.W. Manley, Dec. 29, 1939.